AH-1 COBRA GUNSHIP
VS
NVA ARMOR
Vietnam 1967–73

PETER E. DAVIES

OSPREY PUBLISHING
Bloomsbury Publishing Plc
Kemp House, Chawley Park, Cumnor Hill, Oxford, OX2 9PH, UK
29 Earlsfort Terrace, Dublin 2, Ireland
1385 Broadway, 5th Floor, New York, NY 10018, USA
E-mail: info@ospreypublishing.com

OSPREY is a trademark of Osprey Publishing Ltd

First published in Great Britain in 2025

ISBN: PB 9781472861740; eBook 9781472861733; ePDF 9781472861757;
XML 9781472861726

25 26 27 28 29 10 9 8 7 6 5 4 3 2 1

Edited by Tony Holmes
Cover artwork and battlescene by Gareth Hector
Three-views, side-views, cockpit view, Engaging the Enemy artwork and
armament views by Jim Laurier
Map and tactical diagrams by www.bounford.com
Index by Angela Hall
Typeset by PDQ Digital Media Solutions, Bungay, UK
Printed by Repro India Ltd

AH-1G cover artwork
Maj Larry McKay and pilot CW2 Barry McIntyre, in AH-1G "Serpent 6"
of F Battery, 79th AFA, were heavily involved in the defense of An Loc on
April 13, 1972. Upon arriving over the besieged town with other gunships,
McKay (who was the F Battery commander) reassured Col William H. Miller
– the senior US advisor on the ground – that his Cobras were armed with
HEAT rockets fitted with small, precise six-pound anti-armor warheads that
would minimize collateral damage. Despite heavy AAA, McIntyre flew a
"wingover" maneuver at 5,000ft, dived at an angle of 35 degrees and hit the
lead T-54B in its vulnerable engine bay as the tanks closed to within 1,000ft
of Miller's command post. A subsequent explosion blew the T-54B's turret off.
"Serpent 6" then disabled another leading tank, followed by the last one in the
column, trapping the others. Cobras ultimately destroyed five tanks in this
single engagement. (Artwork by Gareth Hector)

NVA armor cover artwork
This PT-76 amphibious light tank was one of several that supported NVA
infantry as the latter overran ARVN forces defending the small town of Loc
Ninh on April 5, 1972. Six AH-1Gs and three OH-6As of F Troop, 9th
Cavalry responded to the attack, with Capt Ronald Timberlake and WO1 Bob
Stein leading the helicopters into action. They engaged the PT-76, which was
blocking the route into Loc Ninh, with 2.75in. rockets armed with 17lb
Mk 229 high explosive warheads, firing the weapons at low altitude. When
intensive AAA threatened to down the Cobra, a flight of USAF F-4 Phantom
IIs dropped a full bomb load onto NVA troops in an east-to-west direction
across the road into the village, diverting and then destroying many of the
enemy gun positions. (Artwork by Gareth Hector)

Previous Page
With its rocket pods empty, a 1st Platoon, 334th AHC AH-1G Cobra returns
to the unit's forward operating base at Duc Hoa, 20 miles west of Saigon, in
November 1967. Using the callsign "Playboy," the platoon had commenced
combat operations with the AH-1G the previous month. Like the UH-1, from
which the helicopter gunship was derived, the Cobra had its tail rotor on the
port side. On at least 15 occasions the tail rotor yoke failed and the rotor came
away, causing a number of serious accidents. (US Army)

CONTENTS

INTRODUCTION

In a conflict that became known as the helicopter war, the fighting in Vietnam saw the development of many new weapons systems either initiated or accelerated. In the mountains, jungles, and river deltas of Southeast Asia, the helicopter soon replaced conventional vehicles as the primary means of moving troops rapidly, or extracting them from trouble.

By 1971, North Vietnamese Army (NVA) regiments were increasingly supplementing their infantry units with tanks, armored personnel carriers, and artillery. Consequently, US Army armed helicopters, which had been effective in escorting and defending airmobile assault forces, had to face this growing threat, using new anti-armor weapons and techniques. The North Vietnamese invasion of South Vietnam in the spring of 1972 included surprisingly large numbers of armored vehicles, and the US Army's AH-1G Cobra gunships took on a crucial role in destroying many of them. These helicopters had originally been purchased mainly to deal with the Cold War threat of a massive assault on Western Europe by Soviet tank columns.

In Vietnam the AH-1G would fulfill that role against similar Soviet tanks while serving in several other gunship roles. Although most destruction of NVA armor was accomplished by fixed-wing gunships, tactical air power, and

The Model D207 Sioux Scout was a proof-of-concept gunship developed by Bell in 1962–63. The helicopter was evaluated by the 11th Air Assault Division, whose pilots were impressed by its tandem crew compartment. They suggested a larger version be built with more power and capability. (Bell)

B-52 *Arc Light* attacks, the relatively small number of Cobras (and far fewer UH-1B Huey gunships) could hit tanks and vehicles in locations where other aerial weaponry would have caused collateral losses.

The US Army received its first helicopters in 1947. Armed helicopter tactics developed in the years following the Korean War, in which the Bell OH-13 Sioux helicopter had proved useful for evacuating combat casualties. Lt Gen Hamilton "Ham" Howze, heading the Howze Board at Fort Bragg, North Carolina, issued a 1962 report outlining the concept of the Air Assault Division in which helicopters were central. It also formalized armed helicopter techniques initially developed in June 1955 after Brig Gen Carl Hutton instructed helicopter expert Col Jay Vanderpool at Fort Rucker, Alabama, to investigate the offensive use of helicopters. The resultant "Sky Cavalry" unit was later commanded by Col Vanderpool and reorganized as the 7292nd Aerial Combat Reconnaissance Company (Provisional) in 1958.

With an intended speed of 250mph, a four-bladed rigid main rotor and a novel "rotorprop" pusher propeller/tail rotor, the prototype AH-56A Cheyenne first flew on September 2, 1967. It had a helmet-mounted weapons sighting system, a rotating seat and periscope for the gunner's cockpit, and weapons on six external pylons. Here, three of the ten examples built by Lockheed fly in formation for the camera during an air-to-air photo sortie north of Santa Barbara, California. (Lockheed)

The airmobile concept, which owed its origins largely to Howze's work, was later proven in field exercises with the newly formed 11th Air Assault Division (Test) in 1964 and then combat tested in Vietnam when the unit became the 1st Air Cavalry Division. The Howze Board's recommendations included armed helicopters for escorting troop-carrying helicopter formations and suppressing hostile fire around a landing zone for the assault force. Bell's new turbine-powered HU-1A (later, UH-1A) was obviously the appropriate aircraft. With power-operated controls, a throttle governor to maintain constant speed, and unprecedented performance, the revolutionary "Huey" and its gunship derivatives quickly became vital to US Army airborne operations.

Realizing the helicopter's potential as an anti-armor weapon in 1957, Bell equipped an OH-13 with SS-11 anti-tank missiles that same year. Later, more powerful UH-1C Huey gunships fired them. Among the US Army helicopters that arrived in South Vietnam in 1962 were 11 improved UH-1Bs with M6 M60C machine guns and 2.75in. rocket launchers. By 1964 their combat experience confirmed the need for a dedicated "gunship" for airborne assaults.

Armed UH-1Cs of the 1st Cavalry Division were already seen as "interim gunships" as the US Army was anticipating a faster, better-armed helicopter to precede cavalry assault formations and tackle ground defenses. It issued a request for proposals in mid-1964 for a long-range deep interdiction aircraft and escort – the Advanced Aerial

The prototype Model D209, with small doors above its retractable skids. Project leader Mike Folse measured a Spitfire fighter to determine the cockpit width of the helicopter gunship. (Terry Panopolis collection)

Fire Support System (AAFSS). Seven contractors, including Bell, submitted bids, and Lockheed's CL-840 (AH-56 Cheyenne) was selected in November 1965. However, it was an extremely sophisticated "compound helicopter" design combining fixed-wing and helicopter elements and requiring protracted development.

Bell's seven years of gunship development led to the Project D255 Iroquois Warrior mock-up in June 1962. It had a tandem cockpit with the gunner at the front, external weapons on stub wings, and a General Electric TAT-101 twin M60 machine gun nose turret, with a 20mm gun pod under the fuselage. To reduce costs through "commonality" between aircraft variants, many components were shared with the UH-1 Huey. A modified version of the D255, known as the D262, was entered unsuccessfully for the AFFSS competition. The company then began a "scout helicopter" program.

Bell's veteran OH-13 Sioux became a proof-of-concept gunship with a new forward fuselage containing a tandem crew compartment, turreted machine guns, and "side-stick" flight controls for the gunner. The Model D207 Sioux Scout was flown in July 1963 and evaluated by the 11th Air Assault Division, which suggested a scaled-up version. Bell obliged with the company-funded Model D209, promoted against rival projects from Sikorsky, Boeing Vertol, Piasecki, and Kaman as a cost-saving modified UH-1. All four promotions outlined gunships that would be available during the AH-56's delayed development. The US Army clearly wanted another interim gunship as long as it could be delivered "within two years," according to Gen William Westmoreland, Commander, US Military Assistance Command Vietnam (COMUSMACV).

The D209 was duly evaluated by the US Army's Army Materiel Command led by Col Harry Bush's "Bush Board" on August 18, 1965. A team led by noted industrial designer Richard Ten Eyke had completed the prototype within just seven months on a tight budget in Bell's new "Green Room" production area, and it first flew on September 7, 1965 with Bell test pilot Bill Quinlan at the controls. Extended testing at Edwards AFB, California, and at Fort Sill near Lawton, Oklahoma, showed the clear superiority of the D209 over its rivals. By the time of the helicopter's selection for production more than 300 pilots had flown it.

Initially, the new gunship was designated UH-1H, implying a modified Huey. However, that designation was soon allocated to the improved UH-1D transport, and the Model 209 became the AH-1G Huey Cobra. A European promotional tour followed in which the prototype performed admirably throughout, and it was obviously time to plan for production examples to head out to Vietnam, where it would become a tank killer in place of the Cheyenne.

CHRONOLOGY

1947
Spring
T-54A tank enters production.

1950
Summer
Bell experimentally mounts a bazooka anti-tank weapon on an OH-13 Sioux helicopter.

1955
June
Col Jay Vanderpool's team ("Vanderpool's Fools") successfully tests 0.50-cal. machine guns and rockets on an OH-13 Sioux for ground attack.

Summer
NVA forms its first armored company using captured US Army equipment.

1956
October
Bell flies the XH-40, the first turbine-engined helicopter, later re-designated the UH-1 Iroquois.

1958
Fall
Bell outlines the Model D245, a slender, tandem "Combat Reconnaissance Helicopter."

1959
March 28
7292nd Aerial Combat Reconnaissance Company is formed at Fort Rucker to develop the armed helicopter concept.

Spring
NVA receives Soviet T-34/85 tanks and SU-76 self-propelled guns. Early production HU-1As enter US Army service.

1962
June
Bell Project 255 "Iroquois Warrior" mock-up is completed and begins to resemble the Cobra.

December
Bell also works on the Model 207 Sioux Scout.

1963
July
US Army evaluates the armed Sioux Scout.

1964
March 19
3rd Squadron, 17th Air Cavalry is activated at Fort Benning, Georgia, to validate the air cavalry concept, including armed escort helicopters in assault formations.

November
Lockheed's AH-56 Cheyenne is chosen over Bell's Model D262 for further development in the AAFSS competition.

1965
February
AH-56 Cheyenne wins the AAFSS competition but Bell proceeds with its privately funded Model D209. A prototype is completed on September 2 and flies five days later.

Summer
North Vietnam receives PT-76 and T-54 tanks together with ZSU-57-2 mobile anti-aircraft artillery (AAA) weapons.

September 23
A US Army team led by Gen George Philip "Phip" Seneff, a champion of army aviation, recommends the Model D209 after extensive flight tests.

July 3
1st Cavalry Division is alerted for deployment to Vietnam in October.

1966
April 13
Bell is awarded a contract for 110 modified Model D209s, now redesignated AH-1G.

A local Vietnamese artist provided the 114th AHC with its nose art at Vinh Long in 1970–71. This helicopter also appears to have mission tally markings beneath the rear cockpit. [Terry Panopalis collection]

October	First AH-1G (66-15246) is completed and begins tests at Fort Hood, Texas.

1967

August 29	New Equipment Training Team (NETT) with AH-1Gs arrives at Bien Hoa AB, South Vietnam, for the type's combat introduction and crew training.
October 6	1st Platoon, 334th Armed Helicopter Company (AHC) becomes the first operational Cobra unit.

1968

January	235th Aero Weapons Company (AWC) commences combat operations from Can Tho in the IV Corps region of South Vietnam.
February 6	NVA tanks make their first assault of the war, attacking Lang Vei Special Forces Camp.
February	1st Cavalry Division (Airmobile) receives it first Cobras for 1/9th Cavalry and D/229th AHC, introducing "Pink" team reconnaissance tactics with OH-6 scout helicopters in the I Corps area of South Vietnam.

April	1st Cavalry Division AH-1Gs participate in Operation *Pegasus*, the relief of Khe Sanh Combat Base, and offensive operations in the A Shau Valley. Cobras destroy a six-vehicle convoy including a tank.
July	361st AWC, based in the II Corps area of South Vietnam, accepts AH-1Gs.

1969

January	2nd Battalion, 20th Artillery (Aerial Rocket) becomes the first all-Cobra unit in Vietnam.
June	President Richard Nixon announces the reduction of US forces in Southeast Asia. 9th Aviation Battalion is the first Cobra unit to wind down.
August	D Troop (Air), 1/10th Cavalry, D Troop (Air), 3/4th Cavalry, the 11th Armored Cavalry Regiment (Air Cavalry Troop) and F Troop, 8th Cavalry (Americal Division) receive AH-1Gs. 3/17th Air Cavalry, 7/17th Air Cavalry and 7/1st Cavalry convert to AH-1Gs.

A T-54B lies immobilized in southern An Loc on June 14, 1972, destroyed by the ARVN's 8th Infantry Regiment. The graffiti often painted on the fronts of wrecked NVA armor were the names and regimental serial numbers of the individual troops who claimed the tanks' destruction in the hope that they would receive their promised 50,000 piaster (US$50) per tank reward. Cobras were ideal for tackling armor in these confined civilian areas. (AP/Alamy)

September	361st AWC begins support missions over Laos and Cambodia from Kontum.
October	1st Cavalry Division moves to the III Corps area.
Fall	AH-1Gs are at a peak strength of more than 650 in South Vietnam, with additional units converting to the type including the 114th and 187th AHCs, the first Assault Helicopter Companies exclusively equipped with Cobras. Flechette rockets are introduced.
December	M35 weapons system, with an M195 20mm cannon, is introduced. Cobras begin unofficial reconnaissance over Cambodia, supporting Special Forces.

1970

January	US advisors learn that the NVA intends to bring tanks across the demilitarized zone (DMZ) into South Vietnam.
Spring	US withdrawal from Vietnam is accelerated.
April 29	Army of the Republic of Vietnam (ARVN) and US ground and air units begin assaults into Cambodia, including Cobras from the 2/20th Aerial Rocket Artillery (ARA), 229th AHC, 1/9th Cavalry and the 11th Armored Cavalry, attacking NVA vehicles and weapons caches.

June	F Troop, 79th Aerial Field Artillery (AFA) pilots report SA-7 Strela surface-to-air missile (SAM) firings.

1971

January 29	D Troop, 3/5th Cavalry support Operation *Dewey Canyon II*.
January 31	Eight air cavalry units participate in *Lam Son 719*, attacking enemy air defenses and armored vehicles while flying no fewer than 19,235 sorties. More than 65 tanks are encountered in the first major tank versus gunships confrontation.
November	A Troop, 17th Air Cavalry Cobras support NVA forces on the Cambodian border in Operation *23/7* amid rumors of a massive NVA armored advance in Kontum Province.

1972

January	NVA tanks, now 650 strong, appear on the Ho Chi Minh Trail for the first time, heading for Kontum.
January 25	361st AWC Cobras attack two tanks in the Plei Trap Valley.
March	101st Airborne Division is the last US Army division to begin withdrawal from Vietnam, but the F/79th AFA and the 60th AHC remain with their Cobras, together

	with F Troop, 8th Cavalry and D Troop, 1/1st Cavalry.
March 30	Three divisions of NVA forces enter South Vietnam across the DMZ with armor (including 200 tanks), artillery and AAA in the vanguard of the *Nguyen Hue* campaign, known in the West as the Easter Offensive.
April 2	F Troop, 8th Cavalry Cobras participate in the attempted rescue of EB-66 crew "Bat 21".
April 5	NVA 9th Division troops and tanks attack Loc Ninh and F Troop, 9th Cavalry Cobras destroy a PT-76. T-54s appear, terrifying ARVN troops.
April 6	F Troop, 1/9th Cavalry Cobras are tasked with pinpoint attacks on artillery positions in Loc Ninh.
April 11	F Troop, 1/9th Cavalry Cobra destroys a tank with 17lb rockets.
April 13	NVA forces attack An Loc. F/79th AFA Cobras destroy six T-54 tanks with high explosive anti-tank (HEAT) rockets. 229th Assault Helicopter Battalion (AHB) Cobras destroy 21 trucks.
April 14	Cobras attack nine tanks in An Loc.
April 15	Cobras face heavy AAA supporting troops on the An Loc defense lines. High Explosive Dual Purpose (HEDP) rockets become available to F/79th AFA, enabling more tank kills.
April 17	Cobras with AC-130s and tactical aircraft attack tanks advancing on "Windy Hill" firebase near An Loc. Six tanks are destroyed.
April 24	AH-1Gs have now destroyed 12 tanks and damaged six more beyond repair, together with 29 other vehicles. More than 1,000 NVA troops have been killed in Cobra attacks.
May 2	1st Combat Aerial NUH-1Bs with 361st AWC AH-1G escort destroy four tanks with M26 tracked,

	wire-guided (TOW) missiles near Kontum.
May 8–10	There are several reports of SA-7s being fired at Cobras.
May 11	The first shoot-down of a Cobra by an SA-7 Strela occurs near An Loc just after it has destroyed two tanks.
May 12–13	A major NVA night attack on An Loc mainly uses PT-76 tanks.
May 14	361st AWC Cobras, 1st Combat Aerial NUH-1Bs and tactical aircraft attack armor near Kontum, destroying 17 tanks. Cobras fly on every NUH-1B anti-tank mission.
May 15	A D Troop, 229th AHC crew destroy a vehicle-mounted twin 23mm AAA battery and shares in the destruction of a tank with an AC-130 Spectre *Pave Aegis* gunship.
May 16	First sighting of an NVA ZSU-57-2 self-propelled anti-aircraft gun (SPAAG) in Military Region III occurs.
May 16–19	Cobras and AC-130s hit heavy artillery and vehicles 18km from Kontum, defeating a "human wave" attack on the town.
May 24	Cobras attack six tanks threatening the ARVN's 44th Infantry Regiment.
May 28–29	Cobras fire 3,000 rockets in attacks on NVA vehicles and troops.
June 20	Two out of three F/79th AFA Cobras defending ARVN troops on Highway 13 are shot down, one by a Strela and the other by 12.7mm gunfire.
August	361st AWC, 48th AHC and F/79th AFA AH-1Gs return to the USA.

1973

January 16	Final AH-1G loss of the war occurs due to a refueling mishap.
February–March	Remaining Cobra units return to the USA.

DESIGN AND DEVELOPMENT

The Bell D209's immediate success derived from its combination of innovation (and elements of the previous gunship projects) with the UH-1's battle-proven overall structure, at an attractive cost. Around 85 percent of its mechanical components were compatible with the UH-1C. The D209 had the same fuselage length of 44ft 5in., but tandem seating reduced the fuselage width to 36in. Consequent drag reduction assisted in raising the maximum speed to 253mph. Importantly, it was cleared to dive at 218mph, allowing rocket attacks at steep angles. Its drag coefficient was further improved by flush-mounting rivets and antennas and streamlining the rotor mast housing and engine air intakes. Stub wings spanning 10ft 4in. added lift at high speeds

The D209 served as the AH-1 Cobra prototype, and it is seen here on an early test flight. N209J was a company-funded testbed that used the drivetrain and tail boom from a UH-1B to create a completely new helicopter gunship. Note the D209's unique retractable landing skids, which failed to make it into series production. (Bell)

Suitably garish and "scary" artwork inevitably appeared on many Cobras' aggressive noses, including pristine 68-15084 seen at Bien Hoa, in Military Region III, in November 1970 serving with the 334th AHC. This helicopter survived its time in South Vietnam to later be upgraded into an AH-1F. The combat veteran has been displayed within the Air–Land–Space Museum in Las Vegas, Nevada, for a number of years. (Terry Panopalis collection)

OPPOSITE BOTTOM

The gunner's pantographic gunsight (similar to that fitted in the UH-1C) dominated the front cockpit, as can clearly be seen in this AH-1G at Vung Tao in February 1971. Linked to the M28A1 turret, the device controlled the M129 40mm grenade launcher and M134/GAU-2B/A six-barrel 7.62mm Minigun, aiming at any point within trajectory limits of 18 degrees elevation and 50 degrees depression, with a lateral field of fire of 107.5 degrees to either side. (Terry Panopalis collection)

and carried four external pylons. Two pre-production AH-1Gs (66-15246 and 66-15247) were built with reinforced wings, and the first was used to test weapons.

The D209 had drag-reducing retractable landing skids. Tests showed that protruding skids would not interfere with weapons release or the turret's firing arc. Fixed skids meant a slight aerodynamic penalty and a speed reduction of three miles per hour, but this was compensated by the weight-saving removal of the skid retraction mechanisms. Accidental "skids up" landings were also prevented. A power-operated folding rotor system to facilitate air transport was canceled in 1972 also in an effort to reduce weight.

More controversially, an armored glass windshield was replaced by lighter, quarter-inch Plexiglas, for it was thought that its small area was only four percent likely to sustain direct hits. After taking heavy ground fire in Vietnam, early Cobra pilots strongly disagreed. Indeed, the first combat casualty for the NETT in Vietnam was gunner CWO Roger Cameron, who was hit by a 0.51-cal. bullet through the front windshield in January 1968. Capt William Hodges of the 7/1st Cavalry was lost in similar fashion in September 1970.

The UH-1C's durable Model 540 "door hinge" two-blade rotor (turning clockwise) was retained but without the stabilizing bar. It enabled the Cobra to maneuver at high speeds. The rotor's 27in. wide blades used a honeycomb structure to reduce bullet damage. An electronic three-axis Stability Control and Augmentation System was installed, providing automatic damping and enhancing control inputs by the pilot, particularly during weapons firing.

The D209's large ventral fin, included to improve stability during autorotation, was removed but a tendency toward yaw instability remained. This was remedied in later production aircraft by moving the tail rotor from the port side of the vertical fin to the starboard. Early examples were modified, although new tail booms were usually required. The tail rotor drive shaft was enclosed in a fairing above the tail boom.

Recognizing the vulnerability of hydraulic systems, the Cobra had a small emergency hydraulic reservoir.

Earlier development work with the Sioux Scout and Iroquois Warrior projects gave Bell a head-start in designing the tandem cockpit section with its large "greenhouse" canopy. It could not be opened in normal flight, and crews in Vietnam soon complained of severe overheating, exceeding 100°F. An effective environmental control system was installed from 1969. The enclosed canopy caused difficulty in hearing hostile gunfire or projectiles passing near the helicopter, reducing the available time to

avoid ground fire. The transparencies could be jettisoned below 23mph, or broken out with a special tool. A vent ahead of the windshield blasted hot air for rain clearance.

A maintainer works on the Lycoming T53-L-13 turboshaft engine of a C Troop, 1/9th Cavalry Cobra at Phuoc Vinh in 1971. The Air Cavalry's distinctive crossed sabres insignia, seen here on the engine "doghouse," could also appear on the nose or rear fuselage. (US Army)

A full load of external ordnance reduced any aerodynamic advantage, but the new helicopter was still 40mph faster than the Huey, reaching targets twice as quickly as a UH-1B gunship. Furthermore, the AH-1G had double the firepower and could remain on target three times longer – it carried 27 gallons more fuel than a UH-1H, adding 45 miles range, although its gross weight was 9,500lb, which was the same as a loaded UH-1H. Both the UH-1H and D209/AH-1 had 1,400shp Lycoming T53-L-13 turboshaft engines compared with the 960shp Lycoming T53-L-5 of the first UH-1B gunships. With the 1,400lb weight of 48 2.75in. rockets, a UH-1B gunship earned its "Hog" nickname due to inadequate takeoff power.

The pilot/commander managed the AH-1 from the rear seat, with a raised position giving him adequate forward vision. He had full flying controls, instrumentation and avionics, and an M73 reflector weapons sight above his instrument panel for the guidance of rockets or other armament on the stub wings. With the nose turret locked in the forward position, he could also fire its Miniguns or grenade launchers.

The gunner had a pantograph gunsight similar to the UH-1C's. His front cockpit also had basic flight instruments and novel side-arm flight controls so that he could fly to a safe landing site in an emergency. A miniaturized cyclic control was installed on his right side-console, requiring greater effort to operate than the main cyclic mounted centrally on the rear cockpit floor. His controls could be overridden by the pilot. The large canopy transparencies, while offering excellent all-round visibility, inevitably left the crew somewhat exposed. A new ballistic helmet was introduced in 1968 to provide better protection from bullets

AH-1G COBRA

53ft 0in.

13ft 6in.

53ft 0in.

than the standard SPH-4 flying helmet, but being heavy, it restricted head movement in hazardous situations where situational awareness was crucial.

Like the Huey gunship crews, the pilot and gunner in the AH-1G had some armor in the form of quarter-inch steel seats and Philco-Aeroneutronic Ausform armor plate side panels for protection against 7.62mm small arms – the most common threat. An armored nose plate was placed ahead of the gunner. Formed from two layers of light steel alloy, the plates were designed to fragment bullets, while the inner layer prevented fragments from penetrating into the cockpit. Additional boron carbide panels could be raised to shoulder height on the seats' sides, leaving only the crew's lower legs and heads exposed to fire. Crews could also wear or sit on the "chicken plate" strap-on chest armor, which was often too hot and restricting for movement in the narrow cockpit. The total weight of armor was 233lb, including 46lb for the engine compressor, transmission, hydraulics, and fuel system. The lower section of the self-sealing fuel tanks could resist a 12.7mm hit. In combat, the tail boom was the most vulnerable area.

Bell used the Emerson Electric TAT-102A gun turret for early AH-1Gs, pending delivery of the Emerson Electric M28 weapons system. The stub wings could carry various ordnance loads, and they improved maneuverability. Smoke grenades were ejected from a spring-loaded magazine in the rear fuselage for target marking. Alternatively, an M8 dispenser holding 12 grenades emitting smoke of various colors could be attached beneath an M157 rocket pod – useful for smoke screens.

Two more Cobras (67-7015 and 67-7016) were built to production standards following an April 7, 1966 order. Another order, in March 1967, took the procurement total to 530 Cobras following its perceived success and suitability for service in Vietnam.

OPPOSITE

AH-1G 67-15591 *GRIM REAPER* served a full tour with C Troop, 3/17th Cavalry at Di An, in Military Region III, from July 1968 until it was destroyed on August 9, 1970.

Hundreds of AH-1Gs were delivered to Southeast Asia by sea, including these examples aboard USS *Point Cruz* (T-AKV-19) – the vessel was part of the US Navy's Military Sea Transportation Service. US Army personnel are seen here literally unwrapping the helicopters following the completion of the carrier's voyage from California to South Vietnam in 1969. The Cobras were protected from salt spray by the canvas bags. Behind the AH-1Gs are OV-10 Broncos and CH-46 Sea Knights, also wrapped in canvas. (US Army)

TECHNICAL SPECIFICATIONS

AH-1G COBRA

Selling the AH-1G to the US Army relied partly on its 80 percent commonality with the UH-1, but the gunship's original features made it the first helicopter designed specifically for the attack role. For this it had to survive close engagements with ground defenses. Its 38in. fuselage width reduced the helicopter's vulnerability head-on, although the NVA used triangulated gun positions to fire on it from the sides. The narrow fuselage also increased the AH-1G's susceptibility to high side winds when static.

The Model 540's wide-chord rotor design, based on "pitch cone coupling" and "transient torque" technology, allowed the rotor to effectively unload itself in high-g maneuvers without overtaxing the system and inducing negative g forces that would destroy the transmission system. For the AH-1G, this enabled the helicopter to make hard "wing-over" maneuvers at angles approaching 135 degrees, leading to a dive at up to 220mph for rocket launching. The pilot

16

pulled the nose up and slowed to 80mph, rolling almost inverted. He then let the nose drop, made a 90-degree turn and rolled out toward the target. He had to pull out at a sufficient altitude to avoid structural damage, which could be caused if he exceeded the 220mph "red line" speed limit. A direct dive also gave AAA gunners a more predictable target.

Early Cobras had attitude indicators whose gyroscopes were disabled for up to ten minutes by a wing-over dive, disorientating a pilot in poor visibility and persuading him to invert the aircraft, severely overstressing the rotor and transmission. Improved gyroscopes were supplied by 1968.

AH-1G ARMAMENT

The TAT-102A turret in early AH-1Gs housed a single M134/GAU-2B/A six-barrel 7.62mm Minigun with 8,000 rounds, capable of firing either 2,000 or 4,000 rounds per minute, depending on trigger pressure, in bursts of around three seconds, punctuated by a few seconds' cooling time. Every fifth round was a tracer, giving the effect of a "laser" when fired. At 4,000 rounds per minute, all the ammunition could be fired in 30 seconds. Shorter bursts could jam the feed mechanism. The Minigun was often used as a preliminary suppressor while the pilot aligned the aircraft for a rocket attack.

On AH-1Gs delivered to Vietnam from October 1968, an Emerson Electric M28A1 turret with two M134 guns was fitted. Either gun could be replaced by a Hughes M129 40mm grenade launcher, known as the "chunker" due to its sound when firing, with 231 grenades fired at 450 rounds per minute in ten-second bursts. The M129 was angled upwards to lob grenades at a pre-determined angle, but accuracy was variable. The recommended dive angle for grenade firing was 30 degrees, with a short "gun run." An interlock mechanism interrupted fire from the weapons, which could be fired simultaneously. Used for "area fire" rather than pinpoint accuracy, the M129 was never fired against targets at the same time as 2.75in. rockets so as to avoid the latter being struck by grenades. Very occasionally the grenade feed mechanism jammed, causing an internal grenade explosion that destroyed the turret. Grenades traveled at slower speeds than 7.62mm rounds, which meant they exploded on a target just as the Cobra passed near it – when the helicopter was at its most vulnerable to ground fire.

Heavier firepower could be supplied by a General Electric M195 20mm rotary cannon within the M35 armament system, the weapon generally being considered more accurate for ground attack than rockets. This comprised the gun on a mounting under the

Armorers load 40mm grenades for the M129 launcher into the Cobra's magazine – the latter could hold 231 rounds in total. AH-1G units required large quantities of fuel and ammunition at their main and forward operating bases on a continuous supply basis to maintain their rapid pace of operations. (US Army)

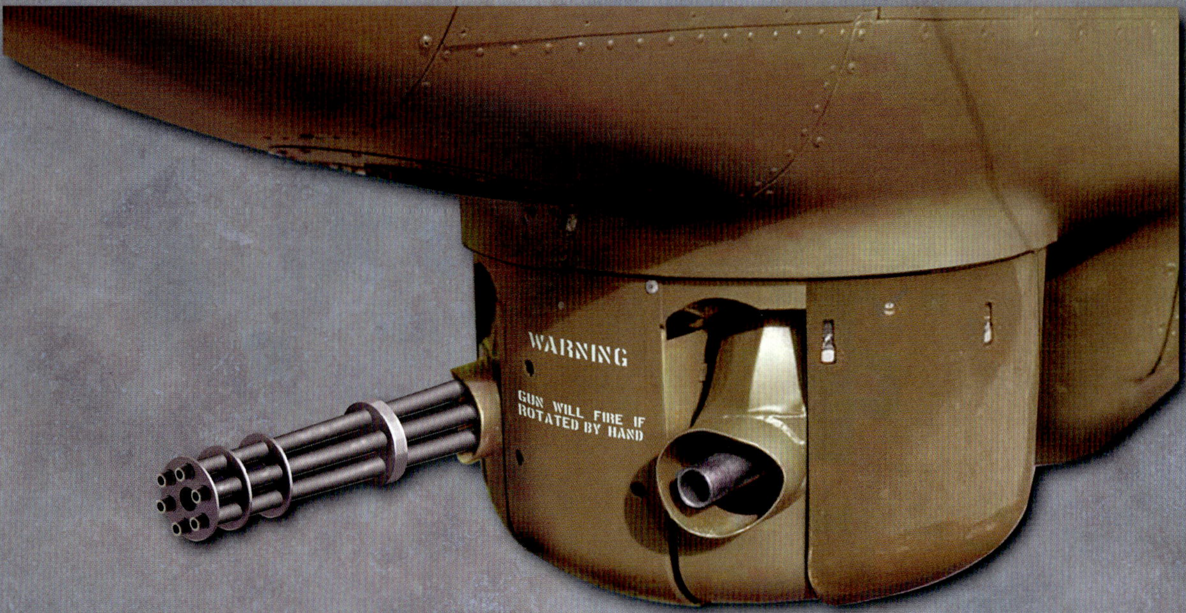

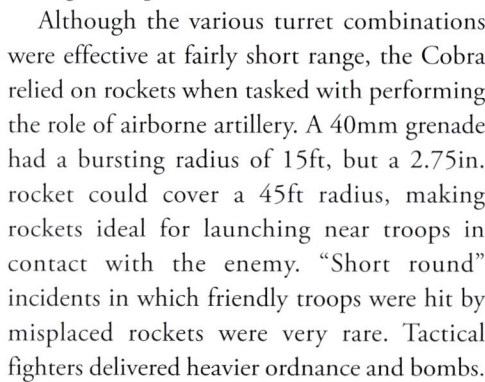

The M28A1 dual-weapon turret, which replaced the TAT-102A, featured a M134/GAU-2B/A six-barrel 7.62mm Minigun and a M129 40mm grenade launcher.

Grenades for the AH-1G's M134 lay on the ramp ready for loading into the launcher's magazine. This aircraft was assigned to C Battery, 2/20th ARA in 1969. (US Army)

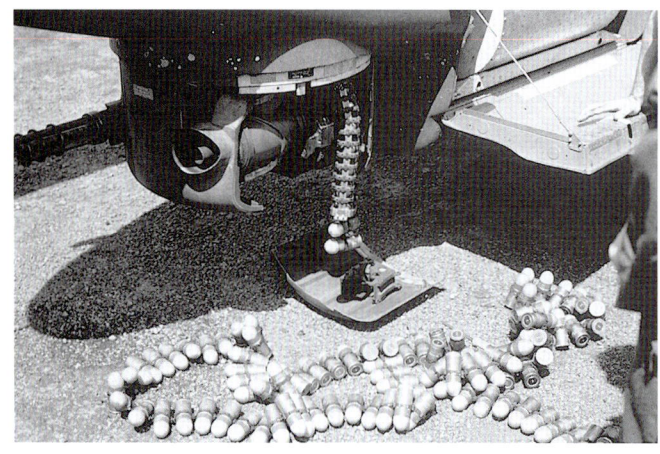

left inboard wing pylon, with a streamlined fairing attached to the lower left fuselage side containing 1,000 rounds. It could be combined with an M18E-1 Minigun pod on the left inboard position with 1,500 rounds. The M195 had a stand-off range of up to 6,000ft, out-ranging the NVA's lethal ZSU-23. Wiring for the M35 system was housed under raised panels on the forward fuselage side. A chute below the cannon ejected shell cases away from the tail rotor.

The 196th Assault Support Helicopter unit had 20mm-equipped AH-1Gs in January 1972, using them to devastating effect on enemy troop concentrations. During the summer of that same year, B Troop, 2/17th Air Cavalry often flew a two-Cobra team that saw one helicopter equipped with rockets and the other with the M195 in missions against vehicles. Some M195s had also been used by Cobras in *Lam Son 719* in January 1971 despite armor-piercing ammunition being unavailable during that operation.

Although the various turret combinations were effective at fairly short range, the Cobra relied on rockets when tasked with performing the role of airborne artillery. A 40mm grenade had a bursting radius of 15ft, but a 2.75in. rocket could cover a 45ft radius, making rockets ideal for launching near troops in contact with the enemy. "Short round" incidents in which friendly troops were hit by misplaced rockets were very rare. Tactical fighters delivered heavier ordnance and bombs.

M157 seven-tube rocket launchers were usually mounted on the outer pylons, with

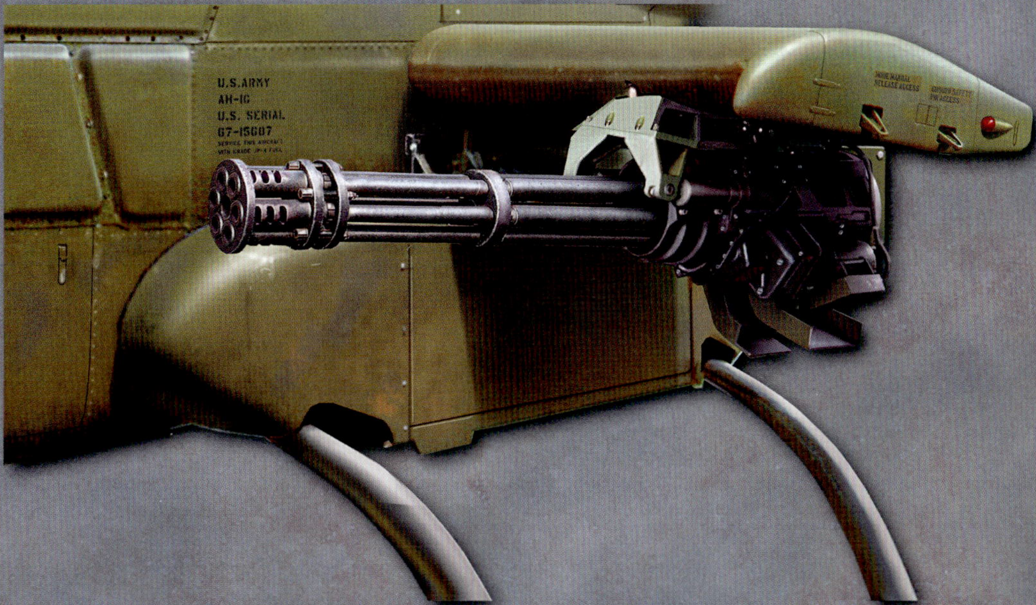

19-tube M159 or M200 "Hog pod" launchers on the inboard pylons. The M158, comprising seven separate tubes, could replace the M157. Four M200s delivered a barrage of 76 rockets, fired in pairs at six per second. In an emergency, the wing-mounted ordnance could be jettisoned at speeds below 138mph, although the inboard stores had to be shed at a 40-degree attitude to avoid them hitting the landing skids.

Each 2.75in. rocket flew at 2,200ft per minute, propelled by a Mk 40 rocket motor. In 1969, rockets with warheads containing 17lb of High Explosive Composition B4

The cut-down M61A1 20mm rotary cannon in M195 form was capable of firing 750 rounds per minute, with ammunition fed via two canisters attached to either side of the fuselage above the skids. Each of these held 950 rounds, as well as the crossover ammunition feed chutes.

An M195 (cut-down M61A1) 20mm rotary cannon unit hangs alongside a seven-tube M158 rocket launcher on this AH-1G. For a four-gun configuration, an M18 7.62mm Minigun pod could be mounted on the right inboard pylon. The M195 was capable of firing 750 rounds per minute, with ammunition fed via two canisters attached to either side of the fuselage above the skids. Each of these held 950 rounds, as well as the crossover ammunition feed chutes. (US Army)

The AH-1G could carry 19-tube M200 and seven-tube M158 rocket pods beneath its stub wings.

and radio-triggered proximity fuses were shipped to Cobra units to supplement the standard "Black Beauty" rockets with ten-pound warheads. With a similar destructive force to a 105mm artillery shell and a bursting radius of 30ft, the B4-equipped rockets were far more effective against "hard" targets including armored vehicles. Their heavier

A rear view of an M195 cannon unit, which formed part of the M35 armament system for the AH-1G. Developed as a result of early combat experience with the AH-1G fed back to the US Army by the NETT, the whole system weighed nearly 1,200lb. Given its combat debut in-theater in December 1969, the M195 cannon greatly increased the effective range at which the Cobra could deal with the enemy's heavy-caliber 7.62mm and 12.7mm machine guns. (US Army)

2.75in. ROCKETS

warheads meant that pilots had to compensate by "lofting" rockets higher to avoid them falling short if they were fired from a range of more than 3,000ft. If rockets had to be fired into wind, preferably head-on to avoid deviation, the pilot could use a high angle of attack to enable them to reach their maximum range. Ten-pound warhead-equipped rockets typically ran out of propellent some 4,500ft from where they were launched.

The success of 2.75in. rockets against NVA tanks during the 1972 Spring Invasion of South Vietnam surprised US Army ordnance experts who thought that far more powerful warheads would be needed. The first tank kills were scored by multiple hits with 17lb high explosive warheads fired from very close range. Proximity fuses meant that a direct hit was unnecessary, but they could prematurely detonate the warhead in trees en route to the target or when flying close to another rocket. Rockets also occasionally collided in flight or flew off course. The Mayor of Saigon was wounded and six of his most senior officials killed by a stray rocket at an air power demonstration in June 1968. If a rocket remained stuck in its launcher after ignition a serious fire could ensue, or the tail rotor could be damaged by debris upon firing.

Anti-personnel flechette rockets also became available in 1969. These were often carried in seven-shot launchers on Cobras' outboard pylons. Each rocket contained 2,200 small, arrow-shaped 20-grain steel "nails" which covered a target area the size of a football field. Red powder was ejected from the rocket body to show when it had burned out at 3,000ft and released its nails. They were useful against targets in the open such as machine gun positions and personnel, although some nails could be deflected by tree cover. However, many would penetrate foliage and decimate any troops hiding under trees. In combat, Cobra crews often had to fire ordnance close to "friendly" troops, but flechettes could not be used at less than 3,000ft from US/ARVN positions.

After the NVA takeover of Loc Ninh, where Cobra crews had been surprised by the volume of AAA and the number of armored vehicles fielded by the enemy, the tactics employed by AH-1G-equipped units changed. Rocket and Minigun attacks, which previously began at 3,000ft in a 20–30 degrees dive, now had to commence at around

Free-flight 2.75in. rockets with either a 10lb "Black Beauty" or longer 17lb High Explosive Composition B4 warhead were staple weapons for all US Army and US Marine Corps helicopter gunships in Southeast Asia. In order to boost their chances of hitting the target, Cobras crews typically launched rockets in salvoes while traveling at speeds of around 80mph. The 17lb B4 rocket proved highly effective against armored vehicles.

This 334th AHC AH-1G is carrying two M200 tubes fully loaded with 2.75in. rockets beneath its left stub wing. The helicopter, parked within its own blast revetment, was photographed at Bien Hoa in the fall of 1967. (US Army)

5,000ft, entering a steep 75-degree dive from almost static speed and rolling out as the "redline" speed was reached.

Rocket firing was timed by an intervalometer, with a predetermined space between shots. If the pilot pressed the firing button less than ten seconds after his previous pair of rockets, the intervalometer bypassed the pair which should have been next. A circuit breaker then had to be re-set to fire the missed pair. In a heavy firefight all ammunition and ordnance would be expended in a few minutes. Two Cobras in a hunter–killer "Pink" team could fire up to 152 rockets and deluge enemy positions with 3,000 7.62mm bullets.

When North Vietnamese tanks appeared during the 1972 Spring Invasion, Korean War-vintage rockets with six-pound armor-piercing HEAT warheads, date-stamped "1953" were shipped to the Cobras' forward bases at Song Be and Lai Khe. Despite their age and occasional unreliability, the warheads were fitted to rockets with canted nozzles designed for launching at slower speeds. They became accurate anti-armor weapons, causing little collateral damage to surrounding buildings. Designed for attacking Soviet armor in Europe, the HEAT warheads required a direct hit to penetrate armor.

From April 15, 1972 the HEDP version of the 2.75in. rocket became available with a shaped-charge warhead like an M72 light anti-tank weapon (LAW), but with more explosives and a wider blast radius similar to a ten-pound warhead. It could penetrate T-54 tank armor, although white-painted HEAT rockets were still more plentiful for anti-tank use. HEDP was also used against AAA sites and vehicles in the latter stages of the Battle of An Loc.

NVA ARMOR

The NVA had armored units from 1955, and by 1965 it had two armored regiments equipped with T-34, T-54, and PT-76 tanks and a self-propelled AAA company with ZSU-57-2s SPAAGs and BTR-40As. From 1965, these units remained firmly in North Vietnam in case of a US invasion. They finally made their combat debut in early 1968 during the Khe Sanh siege, and first appeared in numbers during the *Lam Son 719* battle of January 1971.

The PT-76 light tank was the most numerous in service with the NVA at this time, with 300 available in 1965 compared with 100 T-34-85s and T-54s. The 101st Aviation Battalion was adamant that "the PT-76 cannot be correctly classified as a true tank. It can best be described as a lightly-armored personnel carrier." Its mobility was valued by the NVA and its ability to cross rivers with troops on its deck made the light tank ideally suited to Vietnam's terrain. PT-76s were outgunned by ARVN M48 tanks, although many of the latter were lost to 9M14 Malyutka (NATO reporting name

AT-3 "Sagger") anti-tank missiles or rocket-propelled grenades. The Chinese Type 63 was an improved version of the PT-76, supplied to North Vietnam in 1972 – large numbers of Type 63s and PT-76s were lost in the battles fought that year.

A shortage of armored personnel carriers (APCs) often compelled the NVA to use tanks as infantry transports. Only a limited number of 15-man Chinese Type 63 APCs were supplied from 1963, with these being mainly assigned to the 202nd Mechanized Regiment. Soviet BTR-50PK (based on the PT-76), BTR-152, and BTR-60PB APCs were used in the 1970–72 tank battles. BTR-50PKs carried 12 troops and were armed with a 14.5mm anti-aircraft machine gun.

The lightly armored, amphibious PT-76 was a comparative lightweight at 15.4 tons. It was armed with a 76mm gun and a 7.62mm machine gun in a small turret manned by a commander and loader. The tank commander operated the main gun. The Chinese Type 63 had a similar hydro-jet water propulsion system and a larger three-man turret with an 85mm gun and pintle-mounted DShK 12.7mm machine gun, effective up to 2,500ft.

Seen in September 1967, these BTR-40A anti-aircraft/APC/reconnaissance wheeled vehicles are protecting a supply convoy on the move in North Vietnam. By the fall of 1971, a typical NVA armored regiment contained 40 such vehicles shared between three tank battalions. The APC often served in the same armored units as the heavier ZSU-57-2 SPAAGs, and the BTR-40A's twin KPVT 14.5mm machine guns could be lethal to helicopters. Furthermore, their high top speed (50mph) allowed crews to quickly position them in advantageous ambush positions. (Alamy)

T-54B

A medium class tank, the T-54 weighed 35.4 tons and was armed with a 100mm gun, as well as a flexible 12.7mm and two 7.62mm machine guns. The turret's shape deflected shells and rockets. Capable of 30mph on roads thanks to its 520hp V-54 V12 diesel engine, the T-54 had a 300-mile range. The B-model's Cyclone stabilizing system and Luna infra-red gunsight improved firing accuracy on the move. Licence-produced T-54As were built in China as Type 59s and supplied to the NVA from 1971.

North Vietnam's T-54A/B medium tank numbers had increased to 350 by 1972, followed by 600 more advanced T-55s in 1973–75. The T-54 was a proven, mass-produced weapon with heavy armor over much of its surface. In the 101st Aviation Battalion's estimation, "the AH-1G with present [1971] weapons systems would have little or no effect against a tank such as the T-54." Chinese Type 59 tanks (T-54A copies) appeared alongside T-54s in 1971.

The NVA's first tank was the World War II-vintage T-34-85. Around 100 were still in service for the 1972 invasion, and 60 were destroyed. Weighing 35 tons, this veteran tank had an 85mm gun, although 24 were modified with twin 37mm anti-aircraft guns instead. Heavier 57mm AAA was mounted in a twin-gun installation in a ZSU-57-2 SPAAG based on the ubiquitous T-54 chassis. The NVA had initially

The ubiquitous Chinese-built T-54A, or Type 59, was produced from December 1958 until the early 1980s. This example, probably from the 203rd Armored Regiment, was among several captured by the ARVN at Vinh Phuoc on April 10, 1972 during the NVA's attempt to advance on the city of Hue. On May 2, communist troops, supported by armor, again attempted to surround the city, only to be driven back primarily by massive US air strikes. (AP/Alamy)

ZSU-57-2

fielded only locally built Type 63/65 SPAAGs, based on a T-34 chassis, until 1970, when Soviet-supplied ZSU-57-2 SPAAGs, which entered Warsaw Pact service in 1955, arrived. More than 500 were eventually supplied to the NVA, and they were used extensively during the 1972 Easter Offensive.

The ZSU-57-2 SPAAG's four twin road wheels per side increased mobility on the Ho Chi Minh Trail, where it was capable of 31mph on good surfaces thanks to its powerful 520hp V-54 V12 diesel engine. ZSU-57-2 SPAAGs accompanied NVA forces as a primary anti-aircraft weapon in 1972, although Cobra rocket fire could eliminate the tank's exposed gun crew. The first example was seen by ARVN troops in Military Region III on May 16.

The ZSU-57-2's S-68A 57mm guns were operated by two sight adjusters, a gunner, and a loader in an open-topped turret – protected on its sides by 15mm armor – that traversed at 36 degrees per second. The guns could be elevated up to 85 degrees, firing fragmentation or armor-piercing rounds at 240 rounds per minute, effective up to 28,000ft. However, unlike later SPAAGs such as the ZSU 23-4, the ZSU-57-2 lacked radar range finding or fire control, preventing night-time use.

The Vietnamese-built Type 63/65 SPAAG was purportedly fielded in small numbers by self-propelled AAA companies charged with protecting T-54- and PT-76-equipped regiments committed to the Easter Offensive. The Type 63/65, based on a T-34-76 or -85 chassis, was fitted with a double-barrelled Chinese copy of the Soviet M1939 (61-K) 37mm weapon. This example was captured by the ARVN on August 13, 1972. (US Army)

25

THE STRATEGIC SITUATION

OPPOSITE TOP
At least two NETT Cobras with
TAT-102A turrets were painted
with USAF FS 30219 Tan and FS
34079 Green camouflage in 1967,
and they retained this scheme in
service with other units, including
B Battery, 2/20th ARA. The
helicopter is armed with single
M200 and M157 rocket tubes
beneath its right stub wing, the
latter carrying 15 2.75in. rockets
fitted with 17lb warheads. Aerial
Rocket Artillery units had four
missions – direct fire support,
pre-planned fire missions
(including LZ preparation),
reconnaissance, and escort.
(Terry Panopalis collection)

Worrying indications that North Vietnam intended to use armor in a new attempt to occupy South Vietnam came in December 1971 when huge tank parks were seen in Laos at Hog Back Lake. The previous invasion attempt, mainly by Viet Cong units, in the Tet Offensive of January 1968 had caused considerable damage and losses in more than 100 South Vietnamese cities and US military facilities. US prestige in the area was severely undermined, not least by well-publicized sapper attacks on the American embassy in Saigon and Gen Westmoreland's MACV headquarters at Tan Son Nhut AB. More than 700 enemy troops penetrated the perimeter fences and UH-1C gunships of the 120th AHC decimated them with rockets and gunfire.

Around 84,000 Viet Cong and (in the northern provinces) NVA troops were involved, and their losses of at least 32,000 effectively ended the former's role as a fighting force. The Viet Cong mistakenly believed that the South Vietnamese would rise up and support their insurrection – an illusion which persisted during the 1972 invasion. The Viet Cong's brutal occupation of Hue, South Vietnam's third largest city (regarded as an "open city", with no US Army presence), was a disaster. More than 2,800 civilians were killed by Viet Cong death squads, and mass graves were discovered for many years afterwards.

As enemy forces finally retreated from Hue, scout helicopters of the 1/9th Cavalry tracked them while four Cavalry battalions defeated NVA reinforcements attempting to reach the city. The 7/17th Air Cavalry kept a flechette-armed ("nail bird") Cobra on 24-hour standby to repel "human wave" infantry attacks on Hue. "Nails" were used to destroy 12.7mm gun sites north of An Loc when Cobras in the 1/9th Cavalry covered the rescue of a US general after a shoot down. In February 1968 NVA armored units attacked the Long Vei Special Forces Camp, where tanks were sacrificed to defensive fire at the camp's perimeter in order to create access for the infantry.

Although the Tet Offensive was a military disaster for Hanoi, the extensive media coverage of the damage (including the loss of 142 US Marines at Hue) gave the American public the impression that the US war effort was failing. The domestic anti-war protest movement rapidly increased. In Hanoi, this was carefully observed, and seen as evidence that a more determined future attack on South Vietnam by regular NVA troops with armored support could be more successful. Organizing it before the American policy of Vietnamization (giving South Vietnam the equipment and training to defend itself without direct US intervention) was implemented was seen as vital. Accurate timing also meant pressing ahead before all US troops and advisors had left South Vietnam and closed down their bases and advisory teams. Vietnamization was part of Nixon's 1968 pledge to secure "an honourable end to the war," although the South Vietnamese government wanted the troops to stay.

Hanoi also suspected that the President's negotiations with China and Moscow might result in reduced Chinese support for North Vietnam. In fact, Soviet and Chinese support increased. Crucially, Gen Vo Nguyen Giap, Hanoi's original architect of the invasion strategy, seriously underestimated the US president's willingness to return massive air power to the region quickly. Giap knew that wars could not be won by air power alone, but he did not predict how its support would galvanize elements of the South Vietnamese armed forces. The absence of US troops would mean that a full-scale battle force including armored divisions could be used rather than the guerilla tactics of previous Viet Cong attempted takeovers.

NVA AAA units were highly effective during the Easter Offensive, covering mechanized units as they advanced into South Vietnam. Faced with some of the most intensive AAA experienced since World War II, Cobras crews were engaged by weapons such as this Chinese-built M1939 61-K 37mm gun fitted with a highly effective AZP-37-1M optical sight. Despite the increased number of such weapons in-theater from the spring of 1972, most helicopter losses were actually caused by small-caliber guns. (Dr. István Toperczer collection)

Vast quantities of US military equipment were transferred to US-trained ARVN troops with US advisors, who would not actively participate in combat. The constant expansion of NVA resources and troops in Laos and Cambodia on the borders of South Vietnam, supplied via the 8,500 miles of the serpentine Ho Chi Minh Trail network, was an obvious threat to South Vietnam and

Vietnamization. President Lyndon Johnson had disallowed Operation *El Paso* (designed to close the trails for 18 months using five US Army divisions) in May–July 1966, fearing that it would invoke direct Chinese intervention.

Signs of an impending NVA offensive came in January 1971 with reports of tanks and APCs assembling to the north of the DMZ and in Laos. Several tanks were spotted, but they were unidentified which meant they were recorded as trucks. At this time a fuel pipeline was installed from North Vietnam, through the A Shau Valley and extending into South Vietnam ready to refuel NVA armored forces.

ANTI-TANK DEBUT

The Cobra's baptism of fire in the anti-tank role came soon after its arrival in South Vietnam. On April 7, 1968, OH-6A scout pilot 1Lt Stephen Esch found five trucks and an NVA tank near the Laotian border and called in Cobras, which destroyed all six vehicles. In the fall of that same year, a pair of C Battery, 2/20th ARA AH-1Gs engaged a column of eight T-54s advancing toward An Loc from the southwest. Pilot WO1 Norval G. Brown fired HEAT rockets, hitting several and forcing three to take cover under trees, where the Cobras continued to fire at them. "Pink" Cavalry teams also subsequently sighted NVA armored vehicles.

However, the majority of Cobra activity until the appearance of NVA armor centered on escorting airborne assault formations into landing zones and covering their subsequent recovery. The overall policy of outmaneuvering enemy forces by moving US and ARVN forces quickly into defensive positions, often at first light, or to locations where they could interdict enemy routes, required a massive helicopter force. Gunship helicopters offered the undoubted advantage of being able to identify potential targets on a first pass, rather than making several, as fast jets usually had to do, thereby putting themselves at risk.

An early AH-1G from the 145th Aviation Battalion's 334th AHC heads back to Bien Hoa at the end of a mission over South Vietnam in January 1969. Maj Charles F. Densford commanded the pioneering AH-1G unit as it evolved from the UTT. A Cobra was limited to a half fuel load for take-off with a full weapons load (as seen here) on a hot day. Its cruising speed was more than 40mph faster than a UH-1C gunship, and it could carry 26 more rockets in an ordnance package of 1,760lb. (US Army)

In combating enemy movements of troops and vehicles, a central problem was that this occurred mainly at night. "Nighthawk" flights were duly added to the 229th AHB's Cobra duties. A Huey equipped with a powerful Klieg light sought targets on roads or rivers while a Cobra, with its formation lights taped over, flew above and behind it, ready to attack. Firing rockets at

night briefly destroyed a pilot's night vision, so the gunner had to set up a second attack run.

Cobras were mainly daylight operators, and their important roles required them to be on alert or flying from first light until a third, "last light" crew would take over until sunset. Crew shortages in 1969 compelled many crews to operate these three-shift duties for up to 15 hours per day, with additional night sorties on a rota basis. In 1970 Maj Bobby Briggs, commanding the 114th AHC, felt that "Night operations by aviation units are still in the early stages, but the first indications are that the element of surprise is going to emerge as the most favorable attribute. We now welcome the camouflage of the night." Darkness also favored the movement of NVA tanks, but US Air Force (USAF) gunships were best able to detect and attack them at night.

Negating the North Vietnamese intervention in South Vietnam involved interdicting military materiel traversing the Ho Chi Minh Trail. Fuel and ammunition for tanks and artillery for sustaining assaults was sought out by Cobra "Pink" teams scouring over-extended supply lines. As the following 1/9th Cavalry After Action Report for mid-1970 recorded:

> Enjoying the flexibility, mobility, and firepower provided by the helicopter, the 1/9th Cavalry employed the techniques of modern cavalry doctrine. With the use of the "Pink" team (one AH-1G and one OH-6A), the troops were able to cover large areas effectively. When the situation warranted, the Aero-Rifle Platoon would be inserted to fix the enemy until a larger force could be committed to the area.

The squadron claimed 985 enemy soldiers killed and 464 individual or crew-served weapons captured or destroyed during this period. No less than 579,000lb of rice was also destroyed or seized.

A "Heavy Pink" team with an OH-6A and two Cobras heads out for an armed reconnaissance mission near Phuoc Vinh in 1970. 1Lt John Helms of the 3/5th Cavalry reported that NVA gunners had been warned by their commanding officers "not to bite the little fish [OH-6A] because the big fish [AH-1G] will get you." (US Army)

INVASION

When the Easter Offensive finally began on March 30, 1972, it was timed to coincide with the monsoon so that US air power would be limited by poor visibility. Low cloud levels below 500ft frequently precluded high and medium altitude tactical air strikes, making close air support (CAS) by gunships and *Arc Light* attacks by B-52s necessary to stem the massive flow of NVA armor and infantry. However, flying CAS inevitably put Cobras at greater risk from AAA.

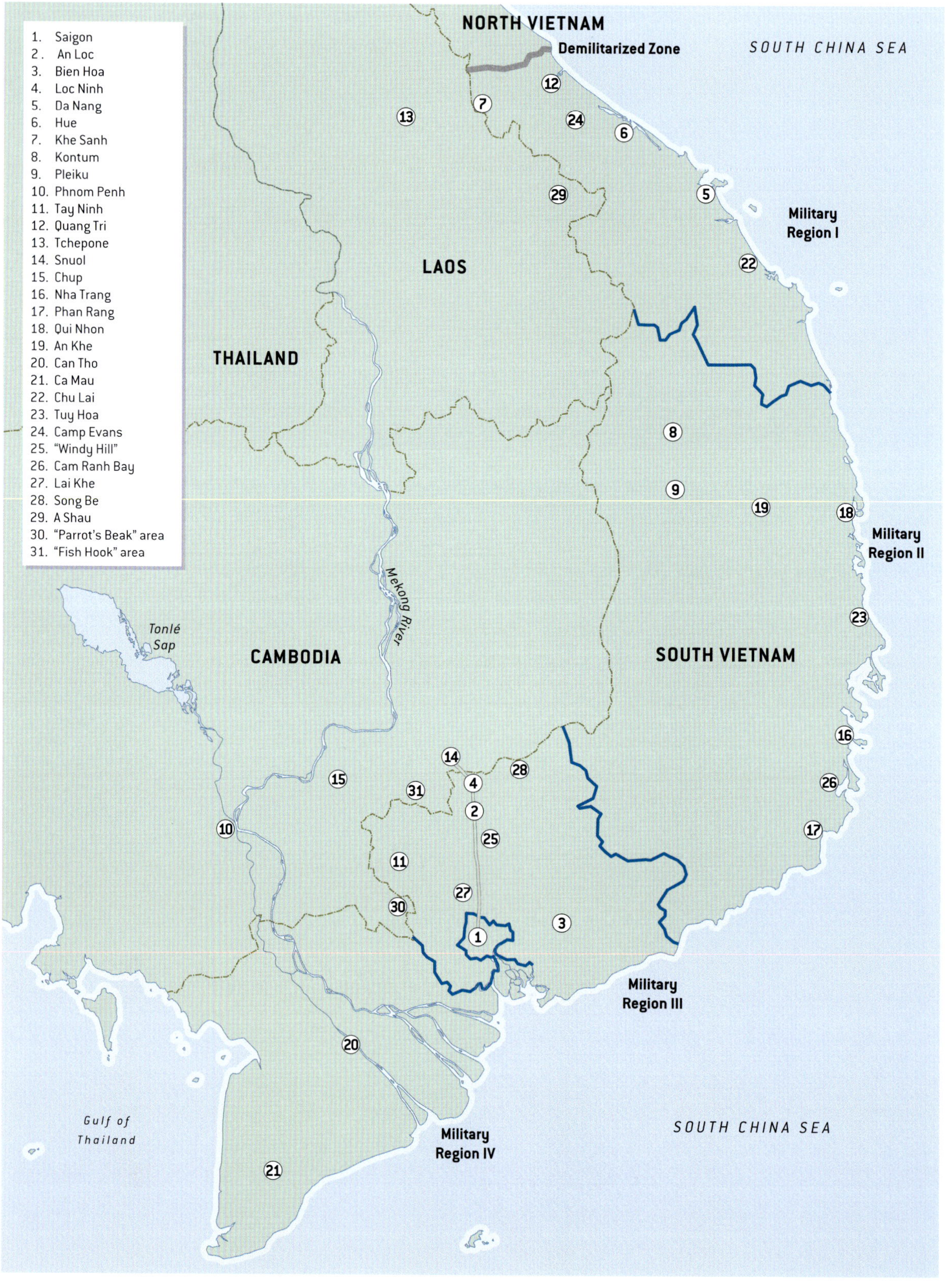

1. Saigon
2. An Loc
3. Bien Hoa
4. Loc Ninh
5. Da Nang
6. Hue
7. Khe Sanh
8. Kontum
9. Pleiku
10. Phnom Penh
11. Tay Ninh
12. Quang Tri
13. Tchepone
14. Snuol
15. Chup
16. Nha Trang
17. Phan Rang
18. Qui Nhon
19. An Khe
20. Can Tho
21. Ca Mau
22. Chu Lai
23. Tuy Hoa
24. Camp Evans
25. "Windy Hill"
26. Cam Ranh Bay
27. Lai Khe
28. Song Be
29. A Shau
30. "Parrot's Beak" area
31. "Fish Hook" area

NORTH VIETNAM

Demilitarized Zone

SOUTH CHINA SEA

LAOS

THAILAND

Military
Region I

Mekong River

Tonlé
Sap

CAMBODIA

SOUTH VIETNAM

Military
Region II

Military
Region III

Military
Region IV

Gulf of
Thailand

SOUTH CHINA SEA

Within hours of the NVA force crossing the DMZ, almost all ARVN artillery positions nearby had been destroyed by tank assaults. More than 140 heavy artillery weapons were seized and used against the South Vietnamese – ARVN troops had little training in anti-tank warfare, for it had not been widely experienced up to then. The NVA's progress from north of the DMZ along Highway 1 (with access to a new fuel pipeline) and from sanctuary areas in Cambodia and Laos depended upon armor being able to use the road network – particularly Highway 13, which crossed into South Vietnam from Cambodia near Loc Ninh, only nine miles south of the border, and terminated in Saigon.

At a meeting of NVA commanders led by Gen Tran Va Tran on March 13, 1972, the town of An Loc was chosen as a potential center for the new provisional government from which to extend North Vietnam's occupation. In Gen Hoang Van Thai's plan the 5th Infantry Division would seize Loc Ninh while the 9th Infantry Division advanced on An Loc. The 7th Division, continuing south of An Loc, would block off Highway 13 to prevent ARVN reinforcements from moving north. By taking Kontum and Pleiku in the Central Highlands and An Loc, the NVA generals hoped to prevent reinforcements from interrupting a complete takeover of the northern part and isolating Saigon and the Mekong Delta area so that additional troops could enter from Cambodia and complete the victory.

An initial feint toward Tay Ninh, southwest of An Loc, suggested that it was intended as a primary target rather than Loc Ninh. NVA generals hoped that ARVN troops would be lured into defending Tay Ninh while the main NVA columns bypassed the town and took Loc Ninh, whose defenses had been closely studied. Knowing that ARVN tanks had taken a toll on their armored divisions in earlier encounters, NVA generals emphasized that they should be destroyed or captured early on. It was assumed that ARVN troops would capitulate in the face of a large-scale armored assault as they had done at Quang Tri.

Another NVA priority was to eliminate two American military advisory teams. Team 47 was emplaced at Lai Khe (a Cobra base) and Team 70 was at An Loc, where senior advisor Col William Miller worked under the command of World War II veteran Brig Gen James F. Hollingsworth, based at Bien Hoa AB. With the cooperation of the senior South Vietnamese officers, they could call in US air strikes and help to organize the ARVN resistance effort.

Foremost in NVA planning was the elimination of the US gunships and tactical air power (TACAIR) that had caused so many NVA losses in *Lam Son 719*. The 271st Anti-Aircraft Regiment was reinforced for this purpose and trained in the use of the SA-7 Strela shoulder-launched SAM – a weapon which would challenge Cobras at medium altitude, forcing them to fly within range of AAA.

Using their *Lam Son 719* experience, NVA planners organized rings of AAA around An Loc. An outer ring at 12 miles gave early warning of incoming aircraft and a second one at four miles had 37mm and 57mm guns. Some well-camouflaged AAA positions, mainly with 12.7mm triangulated emplacements, had been dug in near An Loc as early as January 1969. These had subsequently fired at 2/20th ARA Cobra patrols mounted from Quan Loi, which was only three miles from An Loc. As the campaign progressed and the tank columns advanced on the town, further sites were established closer to the battle – nine AAA divisions were eventually deployed to the area.

Despite the progress initially made by the NVA's mechanised units, MACV claimed that 52 enemy tanks had been destroyed between March 30 and April 4. Forty were victims of M72 LAWs fired by South Vietnamese Marines. Within the first nine days of the offensive ARVN M48 Patton tanks with better fire control systems than the Soviet T-54s had claimed a further 33 NVA tanks, and Republic of Vietnam Air Force (RVNAF) aircraft accounted for 15 more. Cobras began to take their toll mainly when NVA tanks entered urban areas.

The NVA's intention was to take Saigon and move down into the Mekong Delta area (Military Region IV) after capturing several other important towns throughout the country and destroying most of South Vietnam's military capability. The country would be cut in half by taking coastal towns like Qui Nhon, as well as Pleiku and Kontum in the Central Highlands. Attacks on three fronts from across the DMZ in the north, from Laos in the west and Cambodia further to the south would, it was hoped, divide and confuse South Vietnam's military response and undermine President Nguyen Van Thieu's regime. If the three prongs of the assault had been adequately supported by reserves and better coordinated, they might have succeeded in at least one area.

Heavy-caliber weapons like this DShKM 1938/46 12.7mm machine gun – dubbed the "helicopter killer" by American crews – inflicted a heavy toll on AH-1G units in 1971–72. (Public Domain)

However, Hanoi had underestimated President Nixon's preparedness to re-engage with the conflict through the use of massive air power rather than ground troops. By May 1972 North Vietnamese troops were being subjected to 18,444 tactical air sorties per month. Steady attrition of NVA forces as they fought their way from city to city, rather than rapidly progressing to Kontum and then to the coast to divide South Vietnam, severely weakened them en route. This relatively slow advance also gave ARVN units time to reorganize and bolster their ranks, while US air elements were reinforced.

THE COMBATANTS

COBRA AIRCREW TRAINING

The Vietnam War increased the requirement for helicopter crews once the air cavalry principal had been combat proven. Training of Warrant Officer Candidates for the helicopter units became a massive operation in the mid-1960s. Some applicants (known always as "candidates") had previously hoped to fly fighters with the USAF or US Navy but lacked the necessary college degrees. Others just welcomed the chance to fly and serve their country.

Fort Wolters, Texas, was the extensive base chosen to inculcate the challenging art of rotary-wing flight. In 1968 it was extended into Downing Army Heliport, which became home to 1,100 Bell TH-13 Sioux, Hiller TH-23 Raven, and Hughes TH-55 Osage helicopters. The 20-week course began with "Primary One" – an eight-week introduction with ground school and 50 hours in a small TH-55A known as the "Mattel Messerschmitt," with rotors powered by a 180hp Lycoming engine and a transmission allegedly based on seven rubber bands! "Primary 2" introduced formation flight, navigation techniques, and landing in difficult Vietnam-type terrain.

The next stage, at Hunter Army Airfield ("Cobra Hall") in Savannah, Georgia, specialized in basic instrument flying in the TH-13T Sioux. An instrument flight rules (IFR) course extension had to be added for Vietnam-bound pilots. The base's numerous satellite fields had Vietnamese-sounding

Would-be AH-1G pilots commenced their rotary-wing "Primary One" training on either TH-13 Sioux, TH-23 Raven, or TH 55 Osage helicopters, with an example of the latter seen here in the hover. More than 1,100 TH-13s, TH-23s, and TH-55s were based at Fort Wolters and nearby Downing Army Heliport by the late 1960s, as the US Army's appetite for helicopter pilots showed no sign of decreasing. (US Army)

names, including (significantly, in the light of the 1972 battles) "An Khe". Pilots then graduated to the more complex UH-1 Huey for the "Tac-X" phase, mastering assault and fundamental gunship tactics. They learned to use terrain to mask their approach to landing zones (LZs) or targets as gunship and scout crews. Autorotation – the art of landing after power failure by using controlled lift from the rotor – was difficult to learn and led to many accidents.

Bien Hoa became the first main base for Cobra operations from late August 1967 when the NETT commenced combat operations. By April of the following year, when this crew was photographed with its aircraft, the base had survived a series of intense Viet Cong attacks. Early Cobras had dual landing lights in their noses, later replaced by one retractable light. Blue-tinted canopies to reduce the internal temperature slightly in the absence of air conditioning were quickly replaced when they were found to reflect the flash from weapons firing at night. (Terry Panopalis collection)

Training for Cobra pilots at Hunter in 1968 relied on a few instructors with AH-1G experience. It began at St Louis, Missouri, in August 1966 with the formation of the NETT of experienced Huey crews, which subsequently transferred to Bell's Fort Worth, Texas, headquarters. They worked with Bell personnel and early-production AH-1Gs. Having moved to Vietnam in August 1967 and established the Cobra as a viable combat aircraft, the NETT then disseminated its expertise to instructors at Hunter.

The Utility Tactical Transport (UTT) helicopter company developed weapons systems and tactics originated in Thailand and the Philippines in the early 1960s and initially trialed in combat in Vietnam by early UH-1s. Techniques included the use of smoke grenades to mark a source of ground fire that needed suppressing by "light" fire teams of two or three gunships. UTT doctrine was published in a 1965 pamphlet entitled "Twelve Cardinal Rules of Attack Helicopter Combat," which was essentially a handbook for gunship and assault helicopter crews. Many of the instructors for the early AH-1G units being formed at Fort Bragg had formerly served with the UTT, which subsequently became the 334th AHC – the first operational AH-1G unit.

After graduation, candidates applied for advanced training in their selected helicopter roles – heavy lift in CH-47 Chinooks, assault or medical evacuation (medevac) in UH-1 Hueys, or gunship flying in AH-1 Cobras. Allocation of crews to units depended on US Army requirements, and candidates had to accept available offers. By 1969 there were many vacancies. Refresher courses for experienced Huey pilots becoming gunship instructors were in three two-week phases on basic Cobra flying, weapons delivery, and instruction methods.

Although the composition of units in Vietnam varied, airmobile units were based on the Assault Helicopter Company, the Air Cavalry Troop, and the Assault Support Helicopter Company. An AHC had three platoons, two of them equipped with UH-1D/H lift helicopters and a third gunship platoon with AH-1Gs or UH-1B/Cs. The two lift platoons had around 12 Hueys each (or three platoons with seven each) and the "guns" platoon was assigned up to ten gunships, ten scouts, and six or seven UH-1D/Hs for command and control. A Cobra with a Ranger UH-1N Huey carrying an extraction team could be used to rescue downed aircrew. The Aerial Rocket Artillery units of the 4/77th, 101st Airborne Division and 2/20th ARA each had three

235th AWC AH-1Gs dominate the flightline at Can Tho Army Air Field in late 1969. Parked behind the Cobras are UH-1C/Hs. The 235th had commenced operations in Military Region IV in January of the previous year. Cobras and Hueys worked closely together, with the lift platoons flying the latter relying on the "guns" platoons to provide them with covering fire when employing airmobile tactics. (US Army)

Troops or Batteries (A, B, and C) with 12 Cobras. They normally flew in "Heavy Hog" configuration with 76 rockets, and they were managed as artillery units for CAS purposes.

Squadrons within Air Cavalry units in 1971–72 had three helicopter troops and one ground cavalry troop. A troop managed around ten AH-1Gs, ten OH-6As or OH-58As and seven UH-1Hs. In May 1970, the 1/9th Cavalry Division also had three troops each with ten OH-6A scouts and eight AH-1Gs. Four Cobras were prepared for action each day, despite a shortage of trained maintainers. Their task was to destroy NVA vehicles. On many days around ten supply vehicles were eliminated and large caches of weapons were discovered and destroyed. This mission often aroused AAA opposition – a 1/9th Cobra was lost on July 23, 1971 while destroying arms bunkers.

Within a cavalry troop the "Red" platoon, usually the third platoon with callsigns beginning with "3," flew AH-1Gs. The 1st Platoon, with light observation helicopters (LOHs – usually OH-6A "Loaches") were "White," with callsigns starting with "1." The "Blues" (2nd Platoon, "2xxx" callsigns) flew lift UH-1 "slicks." A fourth group, the Aero Rifles Platoon (ground troops), were in UH-1s, ready to cover a downed helicopter crew or recover valuable items such as radios, documents, and weapons from crashed aircraft. "Pink" teams mixed scout and gunship elements, usually one scout and one or two Cobras, with a UH-1D command and control ("C&C") helicopter.

TACTICS

Pilots assigned to scout squadrons had no combat manuals available for the wartime situations they would face in Cobra-escorted teams. They relied almost entirely on the combat experience of others. For Cobra pilots, accurate rocket launching took time and practice. They had to allow for "relative wind" when a helicopter flew forwards without being aligned to its direction of flight, or yawing, thus complicating the rockets' direction when launched.

C Battery, 2/20th ARA AH-1G 68-15089 flies over jungle near the South Vietnam–Cambodia border during a patrol from Bu Dop in the summer of 1970. Cobras usually took off with a combat fuel load of 1,200lb, giving them around 90 minutes of flight time. Clear blue skies and excellent visibility were a rarity in-theater. (Terry Panopalis collection)

Scout pilots, flying at treetop level and sometimes as little as 50ft from the enemy, searched out NVA vehicles, troops, and bunkers. If anyone fired at the "little bird" scout, its pilot called "Taking fire!" and Cobra crews, at around 1,500–2,000ft above and behind him, instantly dived to fire at hostile gunners. Keeping the scout in sight was the chief responsibility of the lead Cobra crew.

The recommended 1,500ft minimum ceiling for gunships was increased to 2,000ft if "helicopter killer" DShKM 1938/46 12.7mm guns were detected. NVA squads often used three such weapons in a triangular formation 3,000ft apart to target helicopters from several directions. Pilots were advised to fly at a 20–40 degree angle-off from the lead aircraft to reduce the chances of a groundfire hit, varying speed and altitude constantly. They avoided flying parallel to treelines, which could contain AAA or armor emplacements, and did not overfly a target and risk being shot down by troops they had just attacked.

Accidentally hitting friendly troops was often the biggest worry for most gunship crews. When troops were in close contact with the enemy, they had to mark their positions or tanks with cloth panels of pre-determined colors. Smoke flares could also be used, but enemy forces often monitored US communications and released diversionary flares. Many beleaguered ARVN firebases relied on Cobras to drive off NVA advances.

During the 1971 ARVN incursions into Cambodia AH-1G attack tactics were modified. Up to seven Cobras flew daisy chain patterns over targets, each helicopter remaining on-station for up to ten minutes. As one helicopter pulled up from an attack the next would be covering it at its most vulnerable point. Escorting troop convoys was added to the schedule. On December 23, 1971, a Cobra escorting trucks to Ban Me Thout took "light enemy fire" and retaliated with rockets and 40mm grenades, although only one casualty was observed. Vietnam experience from 1968 onwards added other responsibilities. These included locating targets for artillery and obtaining clearance for their guns to fire into target areas. Coordination with US Army and ARVN artillery batteries was vital, as shells could enter target areas at the helicopters' operating altitudes. An artillery battery called "Shot" when it fired and "Splash" for the calculated time of impact.

Working with USAF forward air controllers (FACs) or on their own initiative, Cobra pilots could also identify targets for tactical air strikes, manage the strike itself and then provide bomb damage assessment (BDA) after it. B-52 *Arc Light* attacks beyond North Vietnam began in mid-1964, and the 334th AHC, among other units, submitted BDA for those devastating raids. During the battles of An Loc and Kontum, "Heavy Pink" teams monitored BDA for up to 12 *Arc Light*s daily. The lead Cobra crew awaited a "heavy artillery" message on their Guard radio frequency (USAF aircraft worked on different frequencies from US Army helicopters) to warn of an imminent *Arc Light*. Later, they flew in to assess the effect of up to 300 500lb bombs falling into a small area from 30,000ft.

Cobra gunners also had to navigate for scout crews, who carried no maps and relied on "time and distance" and an FM homing device, concentrating on the local terrain for signs of enemy activity. Footprints, disturbed ground water, disguised tank tracks, or recently extinguished cooking fires were among the clues that experienced scout pilots could detect in otherwise normal landscapes. During the NVA Spring Invasion of 1972, many Cobra pilots became scouts in high-threat environments in the search for evidence of enemy tank movements. "Loaches" relied on their Cobra escorts to provide a deterrent presence and deal swiftly with any opposition, although many OH-6As were shot down nevertheless. Sometimes scouts crews refused missions until they could be guaranteed Cobra cover.

Re-arming a Cobra at Bien Hoa in April 1968. Pre-flighting the helicopter, apart from its weapons, was the gunner's task. Both crew participated in "hot" refueling and re-arming sessions at forward bases, with the rotor at "flight idle." This AH-1G has an empty M159 rocket pod and a 7.62mm M18 Minigun attached to its right stub wing. (Terry Panopalis collection)

In 1970 a shortage of Cobra crews forced the 1st Cavalry Regiment to experiment with teams of two OH-6As covering for each other with Minigun pods. A more common modification was the "Heavy Pink" team using two Cobras and one "Loach," or adding a second "Loach." Gunship-related skills came with experience, but US Army policy in 1969–70, whereby Cobra aircraft commanders were rotated after six months, gave little time to acquire the techniques and leadership required. However, the policy also allowed for gunners to graduate to the "back seat" after 300 hrs or three months as gunners. In 1972, several Cobra units had a high proportion of gunners ranked as captains, often outranking their aircraft commanders. Many of those captains were soon promoted to pilot status.

Dive angles for rocket firing depended on the size of the target area, requiring what the US Army manuals called "point fire." A very steep dive at 40–60 degrees from an altitude of around 2,500ft concentrated the fire on a smaller area, or "beaten zone," and could be appropriate for a tank target, but it put the Cobra at greater risk from ground fire. Sixty-degree dives could also be used to relieve troops in contact. Instructors regarded a dive of 20–30 degrees as "steep." "Medium" was 10–20 degrees, and five–ten degrees meant a "shallow" dive.

Rocket firing usually required a steeper dive angle than a gun pass. Steep dives risked over-speeding the rotor and over-stressing the propulsion system in the pull-out. They allowed very little time to align weapons with the target, and generally forced the helicopter to overfly the target, attracting defensive fire. A second Cobra would be ready for a dive attack from another direction. Low-altitude attacks at a shallow angle from a pop-up maneuver minimized rocket aiming time and accuracy, but reduced exposure to groundfire.

1. Master caution light
2. Airspeed indicator
3. Attitude indicator
4. Pressure altimeter
5. RPM warning light
6. Radio call letters
7. Dual tachometer
8. Turn and slip indicator
9. Radio magnetic indicator
10. Vertical velocity indicator
11. Course indicator
12. Transmitter selector decal
13. Go-No-Go placard
14. Exhaust gas temperature
15. Gas producer tachometer
16. Torque meter
17. Emergency collective hydraulic switch
18. Wings stores jettison switch – emergency
19. Compass slaving switch
20. Clock
21. Volt-ammeter indicator
22. Ashtray
23. Fuel pressure indicator
24. Transmission oil temperature indicator
25. Engine oil temperature indicator
26. Air vent
27. Fuel quantity indicator
28. Transmission oil pressure indicator
29. Engine oil pressure indicator
30. Fuel gauge test switch
31. Turret control panel
32. Stub wings stores control panel
33. ARC-54 control panel
34. IFF Mode 4 indicator light
35. Code hold switch
36. Pitot heat switch
37. Temperature selector control
38. Rain removal heat control switch
39. Heat and vent control
40. Air vent
41. 20mm cannon control panel
42. Engine Control Unit decal
43. Cyclic control
44. Caution advisory panel
45. Automatic Direction Finder radio controls
46. UHF radio set
47. Transponder/radar warning set
48. Compass and IFF control panel
49. Door latch handle
50. Pilot armor
51. Pilot's seat
52. Rudder pedals
53. Emergency jettison select panel
54. Stability and Control Augmentation System panel
55. Engine panel
56. Circuit breaker panel
57. Collective controls
58. M73 reflector weapons sight

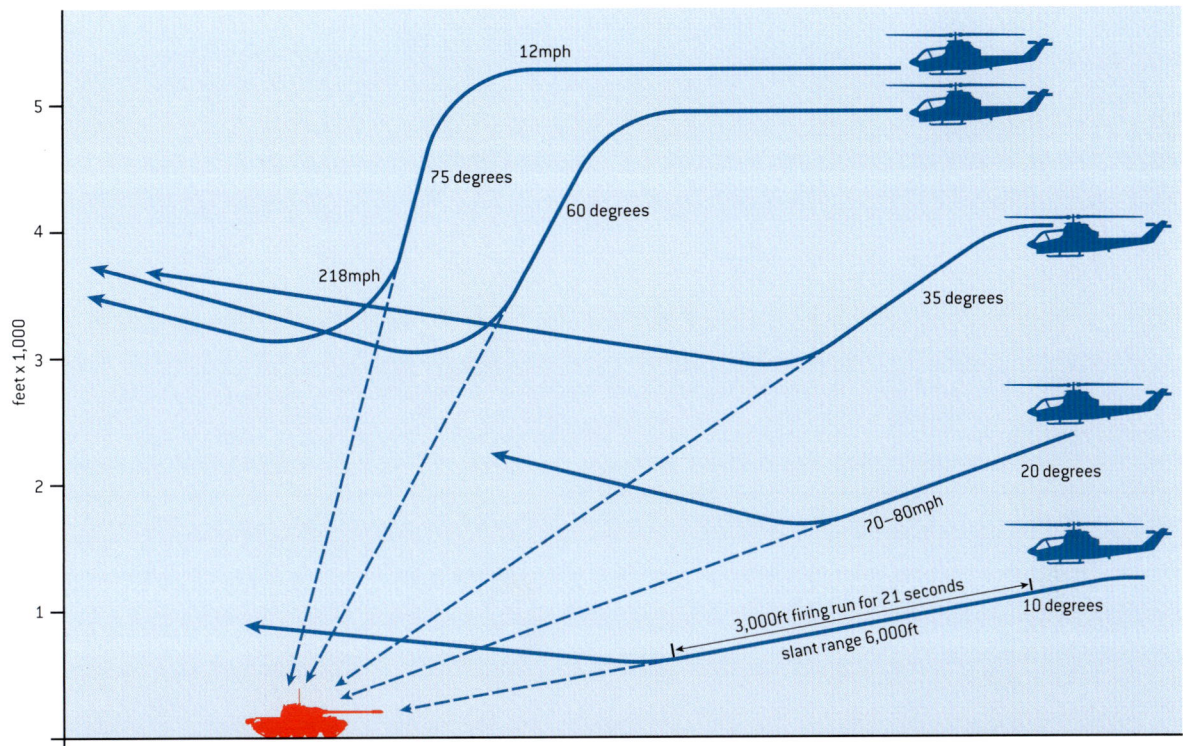

The type of attack required depended on the target and cloud ceiling. Early operations used dive angles of up to 60 degrees. Higher altitudes gave better protection from ground fire where weather permitted them. They also gave greater accuracy for rocket attacks on point targets such as tanks when combined with steep attack angles of up to 80 degrees. However, the Cobra could soon reach its red-lined speed limit of 218mph in a near vertical dive, even when the "wing-over" dive was begun at just 12mph.

ANTI-TANK TACTICS

Gunship training in the late 1960s did not specifically cover anti-armor tactics, as it was thought unlikely that tanks would appear in South Vietnam. However, the syllabus's basic "gun-run" attack profile, used by hunter-killer "Pink" team missions, was adaptable in combat for the tank threat when it materialized. Initially, the Cobra flew a "covering pattern" over the "Loach" at 70–80mph, flying slowly enough to watch the "Loach" but also maintaining sufficient speed to make a quick turn and dive from 1,500–2,000ft to suppress threats that the OH-6A might reveal – it also flew at a high enough altitude to avoid small-arms fire.

Approaching the target, a Cobra pilot accelerated from his "covering pattern" speed to more than 115mph. He could fire two rockets (often called "rocks", they were usually launched in pairs) to distract AAA gunners from the scout. A gun run beginning at a slant range of 6,000ft and leveling out at 3,000ft allowed around 20 seconds to release three pairs of rockets, followed by a five-second burst of 40mm grenades and, finally, about 200 rounds of Minigun fire. Pilots then broke away from the target at a distance of 1,500ft and at an altitude of about 500ft, accelerating to maximum speed to set up another attack run. With an ordnance load of 38 rockets and a full complement of grenades and bullets, this profile allowed for six rocket passes and up to 21 with the Minigun, depending on the nature of the target and the intensity of the ground fire defending it.

The type of attack required depended on the target and cloud ceiling. Early operations used dive angles of up to 60 degrees. Higher altitudes gave better protection from ground fire where weather permitted and greater accuracy for rocket attacks on point targets such as tanks when combined with steep attack angles of up to 80 degrees. However, the Cobra could soon reach its "red-lined" speed limit of 218mph in a near vertical dive, even when the "wing-over" dive began at just 12mph.

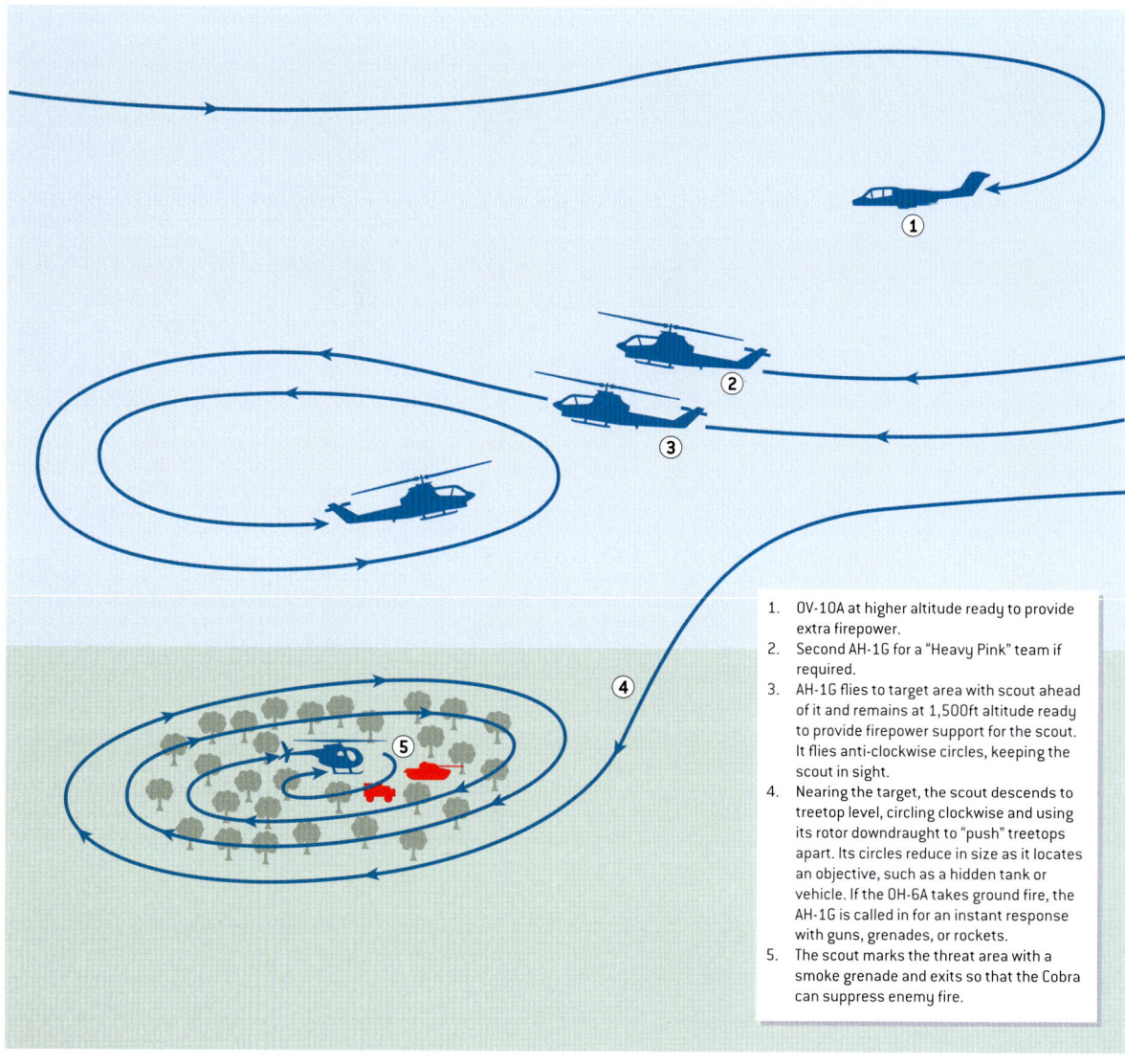

1. OV-10A at higher altitude ready to provide extra firepower.
2. Second AH-1G for a "Heavy Pink" team if required.
3. AH-1G flies to target area with scout ahead of it and remains at 1,500ft altitude ready to provide firepower support for the scout. It flies anti-clockwise circles, keeping the scout in sight.
4. Nearing the target, the scout descends to treetop level, circling clockwise and using its rotor downdraught to "push" treetops apart. Its circles reduce in size as it locates an objective, such as a hidden tank or vehicle. If the OH-6A takes ground fire, the AH-1G is called in for an instant response with guns, grenades, or rockets.
5. The scout marks the threat area with a smoke grenade and exits so that the Cobra can suppress enemy fire.

A standard "Pink" team consisted of an AH-1G Cobra and an OH-6A Cayuse, but two Cobras could be included for a "Heavy Pink" team if the situation required this. The Cobra gunner had to keep the OH-6A "Loach" constantly in sight. If the latter took ground fire, the Cobra pilot dived from 1,500–2,000ft to provide immediate Minigun or grenade fire while the scout pilot exited the area.

A pair of Cobras would attempt to cover each other, firing sparingly to divert AAA and pick off enemy gunners. Typical targets required around four pairs of rockets, while ARA Cobras could sometimes release an entire broadside of 60 rockets in one run against a challenging target. In "Eagle" flights from November 1970, "Pink" teams coordinating with ground troops made evening road reconnaissance flights. All normal traffic was halted to give Cobras a free fire area to destroy any vehicles or armor they discovered. Sometimes "packs" of Cobras without scouts would work with artillery against pre-selected "hard" targets or armor. Traffic on the Ho Chi Minh Trail ran mostly at night, and Cobras, working with AC-130 Spectre gunships or tactical fighters, destroyed many convoys.

Tactics were revised rapidly when tanks and significantly increased AAA appeared in April 1972. Although operational altitudes were raised, some gun runs were made at treetop level against heavily defended targets or tanks. Despite "Pink" teams not

A pair of 2.75in. rockets is released from a Cobra's M200 pod, the latter being boresighted with the gunship's pitch angle at zero degrees. Pilots who were dual-qualified on Hueys and Cobras had to remember that rocket firing in the latter helicopter required the use of the right-hand fingers which usually operated the radio in a UH-1. (US Army)

operating in the same way as they had done prior to the Easter Offensive, scout helicopters remained overhead the frontline, but outside the "hottest" AAA zones. They could make a single low-level pass to gain basic target information and then circle close by, ready to recover downed crews. From mid-May 1972 some missions omitted a scout due to the OH-6A's vulnerability to AAA. Two Cobras were used, with one as a low-altitude scout, ready with instant retaliation against a target. A "C&C" UH-1H flew high to receive reports from the "low" Cobra and obtain permission for an immediate attack.

MAINTENANCE

By October 1972 the 101st Aviation Battalion reported that Cobras were presenting their most critical maintenance problems, exacerbated by spares shortages. Rotor heads, swashplates for adjusting the rotor angle, hydraulic servos, and engine parts needed frequent replacement. After each mission rocket tubes and guns had to be cleaned out and reloaded – reusable metal pods were often replaced with USAF compressed paper types, which could also be reused but were degraded by rain.

Clean AH-1G 69-1642 *SNAKE SIX NINE* is seen in a hangar at Vung Tao undergoing routine maintenance in February 1971. Fitted with an M35 20mm gun system, the helicopter wears the insignia of the Cobra Transition School at Vung Tao on its engine "doghouse." Classes of 24 aircrew were trained by Cobra instructors under Maj Raymond C. Colson's command, with 400 qualified by October 1969. (Terry Panopalis collection)

Natural hazards were added to the maintainers' challenges, including green moss in the jet fuel that blocked fuel filters and engine speed governors. High combat hours were the main source of wear, however. Often, a troop with only nine Cobras was required to have six aircraft available at all times to equip three "Heavy Pink" teams for sustained combat. Very few scouts survived undamaged long enough to reach their 100 hours maintenance inspection. Upon their return to the USA, almost all of the 17th Air Cavalry's Cobras were sent away for rebuilding.

MISSIONS

Cobras, with appropriate armament, could be deadly against tanks. In many cases, though, their mission was to find tanks, eliminate their infantry support with rockets and maintain contact with them until tactical fighter-bombers were called in to drop heavier ordnance. If TACAIR was unavailable, a Cobra engaged the tanks with its limited ordnance. As the 101st Aviation Battalion's report on Operation *Lam Son 719* commented:

> Between 8 February and 24 March 1971 the Cav sighted 66 tanks, destroyed (burned) six and immobilized eight. The majority of the other tanks were turned over to the USAF. Three of the destroyed tanks were hit with flechettes, HE and WP [white phosphorous rockets] and the other three were destroyed by combinations of flechettes, HE, WP and HEAT.

In stark contrast to the Cobra Transition School AH-1G seen on the previous page, 67-15816 *SATAN 10* of the 1st Platoon, 235th AWC reveals clear signs of the wear and tear inflicted on helicopter gunships flying near daily low-level sorties with frontline units. Photographed on the ramp at Can Tho between missions in the fall of 1969, the Cobra was resprayed not long after this shot was taken. (US Army)

Cobra crews received their "scramble" orders from the Corps HQ via the Battalion Operations Centre (BOC), the two five-minute alert crews running to their helicopters. Prior to strapping in, one crew member phoned the BOC for mission details, coordinates and callsigns before boarding his own Cobra for take-off. Capt Robert Metzger noted that "These scramble missions are never routine. When we're sent out on a scramble it's usually because someone out there is getting killed".

En route, they checked for clearance from US artillery batteries while the back-up 30-minute alert team moved into the five-minute alert slot. Nearing the target, they came under the control of a USAF FAC or a "C&C" UH-1H for final targeting details. For many support missions "Snake" pilots took off with their Cobras at excess weights, carrying maximum fuel and weapons. This was usually possible only in the early morning before daytime heat made even a basic hover difficult at military weights.

Weather was a constant challenge to helicopter flyers, particularly over high ground. Gunship pilots usually worked to minima of a 1,000ft ceiling and 5,000ft visibility, but emergency callouts often required them to cope with far worse conditions, such

as 200ft minimum altitude and a half-mile visibility. Missions could vary from preparing LZs with "area fire" to relieving troops in danger of being overrun or covering rescue attempts.

As well as direct attacks on specific targets ("point fire") such as armored vehicles, Cobras destroyed logistics and storage supply bunkers for the NVA's short-ranged tanks. While small 7ft x 5ft bunkers were used as troop hideouts, larger ones contained ammunition, fuel, food, and supplies. Scout pilots became skilful at detecting them, and Cobras could then destroy the bunkers with rockets or summon M48 tanks to fire "cluster" shells into them at point-blank range. Cobras also provided cover for US and ARVN armored columns that began to successfully engage NVA tanks. While NVA columns generally relied on roads, the tactics employed by mechanized US and ARVN units required crews to approach targets such as enemy base camps over rough terrain. APCs followed behind them, while "Pink" teams flew overhead searching for targets.

Cover for medevac (or "Dust-Off") UH-1s was one of the more demanding missions, often requiring two Cobra crews to remain close to sources of enemy groundfire while a medevac team attempted to extract wounded crewmen from under the noses of hostile forces who fired at ambulance helicopters. In early 1969, Cobra units, including the 20th ARA, were allocated many missions in support of special forces Long Range Reconnaissance Patrols (LRRPs or "lerps") deep into enemy territory. As Capt Robert Anderson of the 334th AHC commented, "By far the most rewarding mission is being called on to get some 'ground pounders' like the LRRPs out of a tight spot. They are so small in number that if they are discovered they usually need us to keep Charlie off their backs until we can get a slick in to evacuate them."

SCOUTS

The scout or LOH was essential to Cobra gunship strategy, and the Hughes OH-6A Cayuse ("Loach") was ideal for detecting targets from very low altitude and calling in Cobras to destroy them. They fought at altitudes between 50–100ft, popularly known as the "dead man's zone." Some units, notably the 3/17th Air Cavalry, used the Bell OH-58A Kiowa, but it was considered underpowered.

Built around a protective A-frame roll cage, the OH-6A's egg-shaped forward fuselage would shed its skids, tail boom and rotor in a crash landing and roll over. To detect the enemy beneath triple-canopy jungle, pilots could use their rotor

OH-6A 67-16149, possibly from D Troop, 1/4th Cavalry, represents the "killer egg" scout that was an essential component in the majority of Cobra missions. No fewer than 658 "Loaches" were lost in combat and 297 in accidents during the conflict in Vietnam. (US Army)

downdraught to separate tree cover, risking additional groundfire. For defense, the "Loach" had a Minigun and a flexibly mounted M60 machine gun. Cobras sometimes had difficulty keeping up with the faster OH-6A, which also possessed extraordinary maneuverability, turning within only 34ft.

A "Loach" flew to its area of operations with its Cobra escort flying to its right. Approaching a suspected target, the scout pilot dropped from around 1,500ft to the lowest possible "nap of the earth" altitude, avoiding potential groundfire. Flying above and behind him, the Cobra directed the "Loach" to the target at around 60mph, maneuvering to avoid groundfire. The OH-6A crew chief held a red smoke grenade, ready to mark the Cobra's aiming point. Over the target area or LZ, the "Loach" began a series of rapid clockwise circuits (because the pilot sat on the right side of the cockpit), slowing if no-one shot at it and eventually entering a hover. The Cobra pilot orbited anti-clockwise at around 1,500ft, allowing him room to run in and fire his rockets. While orbiting, the Cobra gunner (or "X-ray") focused particularly hard on the "Loach", ready to initiate a firing pass. If he lost sight of the "little bird," he could ask the three-man scout crew to drop a smoke marker.

As few as two or three rounds from an NVA 12.7mm heavy machine gun could knock out the "Loach's" engine or kill crew members who sat virtually unprotected in the glass bubble nose or open cabin – doors were usually removed to expedite a quick exit in a crash. Scout pilot Lt (later Lt Col) Hugh L. Mills Jnr of D/4th Cavalry was famously shot down 16 times and survived. Fellow scout crewmen Capt Rod Willis and WO1 Ken Stormer of D/16th Cavalry, protecting an ambushed platoon near Phu Loi, were shot down three times during the same engagement. They survived each crash-landing, climbed into replacement "Loaches" and continued the fight. When AAA became too heavy for OH-6A operations during the 1972 Easter Offensive, all-Cobra "Heavy Pink" teams were used, with the AH-1Gs often being flown by dual-qualified OH-6A pilots.

NVA TANKS

In October 1971 an NVA regiment contained three tank battalions totalling 40 PT-76s, 40 T-54s and 40 BTR armored personnel carriers. Each battalion managed 38 active tanks, using ten or fewer for an attack. During the Easter Offensive they were usually far from maintenance facilities, which, together with combat losses, reduced their operational numbers. In the latter stages of that conflict at Kontum in the early summer of 1972, only around 20 percent of the heavy armor remained available.

Prior to the start of the Easter Offensive, the NVA had about 3,000 tank crewmen that had been trained in Soviet tactics at the Kiev Military Academy (formerly the Odesa Tank School) in the previous six months. Their commanders avoided the standard Soviet blitzkrieg approach to tank warfare. They advanced slowly, and were often stationary when they fired at targets. This made NVA tanks easier prey for aircraft. Essentially, the North Vietnamese lacked experience in tank warfare, unlike the ARVN's American advisors.

Furthermore, without airlift capacity to re-supply tank-equipped units, the NVA's logistics chain became too extended and unreliable to support complex armored operations. Its supply lines were constantly interdicted by US air power. Moving further into South Vietnam meant steadily extending supply lines, resulting in ammunition and fuel becoming harder to provide. Although diesel fuel came via a pipeline snaking through the Ho Chi Minh Trail to numerous depots, significant reserves were needed as heavy tanks like the T-54 burned a gallon per mile. At An Loc most tanks entered battle without extra fuel drums attached, and some were simply abandoned when their fuel ran out.

Many of the crews in the T-54s sent against Kontum in May–June 1972 were around 18 years old, and they had received little more than a year's training before being sent down the Ho Chi Minh Trail to the Central Highlands of Vietnam. Machine gunners manning 12.7mm weapons in tank turrets received some instruction in firing at helicopters. They were told to "concentrate the fire on the one that flies very low," recommending "an offensive momentum." Cobra crews avoided flying at 100mph near targets as they had heard that NVA gunners had been trained to "lead" a target at that speed when aiming their weapons, firing one helicopter's length in front of an AH-1G or UH-1. They understood that North

Attracting the attention of Quang Tri citizens, this T-54A was captured on April 10, 1972 near Dong Ha. Eight days earlier, ARVN 20th Tank Squadron M48A3 Pattons had frustrated an NVA armored assault across the DMZ in the direction of the Dong Ha River bridge, knocking out the six leading tanks with their longer-range guns. Nine more were destroyed by RVNAF A-1 Skyraiders. (AP/Alamy)

Vietnamese gunners had been offered a $10,000 bonus for every gunship pilot they killed. ARVN troops were offered less generous bonuses for the destruction of NVA tanks, although promotion became easier following success.

NVA troops called Cobras "Ca Lep" (a type of fish), and noted that the helicopter could launch surprise attacks at low altitude but avoided flying at altitudes between 250–1,100ft in order to reduce the risk of being hit by AAA. Its firepower was "strong" compared with the UH-1, according to an NVA training manual, but it could be "hit at the critical point, that is, the front of the helicopter at the engine room under the main blade" with "armor-piercing bullets" from "any type of infantry firearms." Cobra pilots actually tried to remain above 5,000ft to avoid AAA.

AAA, rather than a tank's primary or secondary weapons, posed the greatest threat to Cobra teams. As a 2/17th Air Cavalry report on *Lam Son 719* commented:

> The anti-aircraft weapons faced can hardly be classified as technically sophisticated, with many bearing design and manufacture dates in the late 1930s. Yet by sound technical deployment and aggressive techniques, the enemy was effectively able to limit our observation ability with the OH-6A because of its inability to survive hits from anything other than small-caliber weapons.

"Pink" teams often called in tactical jets to strike any AAA sites featuring 12.7mm guns or larger. During *Lam Son 719*, 2/17th Air Cavalry Cobras detected three

A ubiquitous DShKM 1938/46 12.7mm "helicopter killer" heavy machine gun in what appears to be a training session for its crew. (Dr. István Toperczer collection)

12.7mm positions set up to intercept incoming UH-1H lift crews. They called in F-4 Phantom IIs, which destroyed the gun positions only 45 seconds after the Cobras had located them.

A highly mobile NVA 12.7mm AAA team of 12 men had two guns, 82mm mortars and two rocket launchers to set up as close as possible to helicopter landing sites. By only firing short bursts at passing helicopters, they avoided having their position pinpointed. Machine guns caused the majority of Cavalry helicopter losses in the *Lam Son 719* battles of 1971. Against assault formations of Hueys, the gunners concentrated on one aircraft (often the leader) or a gunship, and moved their aim to a second once it had been shot down.

Once in South Vietnam, NVA tanks used roads rather than making American-style surprise attacks across open country. Crews knew about M72 LAWs but were reassured that the ARVN soldiers would be too scared to fire them and would run away. They had received lectures on the coordination of infantry and armor but had no practical training or experience of those tactics. They were instructed to move slowly toward enemy lines, with two tanks leading each battalion, rather than in a maximum speed charge as ARVN tank crews had been taught to perform. The lead NVA tanks would then be followed by a second wave to widen out the incursion and overwhelm the defenses.

NVA infantry accompanying tank columns usually carried AK-47 automatic weapons and RPG-2 or RPG-7 rocket launchers. They acted independently of tank crews and were not in position to take out South Vietnamese troops equipped with M72 LAWs ahead of the tanks, which could have then targeted ARVN defensive bunkers and artillery from a distance. For assaults on cities, the policy was "tien phao hau xung" ("first artillery, then tanks and infantry"). At Kontum, tank drivers sought to camouflage their vehicles by day and emerge for night attacks. However, scout helicopters could usually see their track marks and locate them for attack.

In some of the wrecked tanks in the streets of An Loc (and earlier at Binh Long) reporters stated crews were found chained to their positions. They heard from captives that the crewmen had been given stimulant drugs to sustain their energy. Two tanks, destroyed by a B-52 attack on April 16, 1972, did contain bodies of chained crew. Stories of North Vietnamese and Viet Cong troops being chained to their weapons dated back to 1966, when a FAC visited the "body count" from a Viet Cong action. Several deceased gunners were found chained to 12.7mm guns, and NVA propaganda claimed that they had volunteered to be chained to demonstrate their commitment.

COMBAT

The first six AH-1Gs left Fort Worth on August 28, 1967 for shipment to Vung Tao, near the South Vietnamese capital Saigon, before moving to Bien Hoa shortly thereafter to replace UH-1C gunships in Air Cavalry units. An initial combat sortie occurred on September 4 when Maj Gen George Seneff, a pioneer in the Cobra's service initiation and commander of the 1st Aviation Brigade, took AH-1G 66-15259 *Virginia Rose* on a test flight from Bien Hoa with gunner CWO J. D. Thomson. En route, they entered a firefight between UH-1 gunships and Viet Cong on a river island. When the enemy attempted to escape by boat, Seneff sank a sampan with rockets and gunfire, scoring the Cobra's first combat success.

Bien Hoa housed the NETT's Cobras, which were commanded by Maj Paul Anderson from the 334th AHC – in 1961, it had been the only US Army unit in-theater with armed helicopters. The 334th had been the logical choice to introduce the Cobra to combat, with Anderson undertaking the first AH-1 flight in Vietnam on August 31, 1967. The unit subsequently delivered a devastating onslaught when Viet Cong invaders flooded through Bien Hoa's perimeter fences during the early hours of January 31, 1968, killing more than 1,300. Several AH-1Gs had twin turret Miniguns and single weapons under each stub wing, giving 20 seconds of firing time. Intervention by one Cobra, or two in a "light fire" team, could often frustrate a base invasion.

Night missions were frequently required, although the Cobra was not suitably equipped. The Viet Cong regularly mounted nocturnal sapper and rocket attacks on US bases, which meant Cobra crews had to remain on alert ready to repel invaders. Three AH-1Gs were seriously damaged by sappers on November 15, 1969 at Camp Radcliff. Using flares, pilots could also try to identify the sources of rocket firing, which could be primitive truck-mounted launchers ten miles from the base.

First Combat Kill

BELL AH-1G
HueyCobra
AH-1G 15283

1 Sempan destroyed
4 VC KIA

1100 hours 4 Sep 1967
10 miles NE Can Tho, VN

This Bell pamphlet was produced by the company shortly after the Cobra had engaged the enemy for the first time in Southeast Asia. It highlighted the success credited to Maj Gen George Seneff on September 4, 1967. (Bell)

When NVA forces were reportedly massing troops and armor just north of the DMZ in early January 1970, the 2/17th Air Cavalry investigated. On January 3 an NVA supply truck convoy was sighted travelling from Laos, but the tanks remained in place. Based at Camp Eagle, home of the 101st Airborne Division near Phu Bai and Hue, the 2/17th was familiar with operations in this B4 military zone bordering the DMZ. The squadron was prepared to meet tanks, having brought I Corps' entire stock of HEAT rockets with it. Although crews had not trained for HEAT, they knew that tanks had to be hit from the rear or in the engine bay where their armor was thinner than at the front. Alternative loads, used initially by Cobras from Long Thanh, included 17lb rockets on the inboard pylons and flechettes outboard.

Cobras from the 2/17th Air Cavalry, 4/77th ARA and 158th Aviation Battalion were among 100 helicopters involved in several large-scale operations to intercept frequent NVA convoys from Laos into the A Shau Valley. In Operations *Delaware* (April–May 1968) and *Apache Snow* (May–June 1969), UH-1B gunships, Hueys, and OH-6As were used against the formidable A Shau AAA defenses, which inflicted heavy losses on all three types. Ap Bia Mountain, known later as "Hamburger Hill" after the disastrous losses incurred there, was covered in gun positions. Cobras from a forward base at Currahee were particularly effective in firing rockets accurately into the bunkers and "spider holes" occupied by gunners of the NVA's 29th Regiment. In a rocket-launching dive, executing the correct pull-out altitude was crucial. Many pilots, concentrating on their targets, asked their gunners to call out the helicopter's altitude at 100ft intervals.

During the intense battles of 1971–72, Cobras were frequently called upon to save ARVN troops from being overrun by NVA forces, often attacking in "human waves." This required considerable accuracy in dispensing ordnance close to friendly forces, and Cobra crews soon gained a reputation for this skill. Gunships would not fire from positions above friendly forces to avoid exposure to enemy weapons. Also, having

Cobras' cartridge cases and rocket debris falling on them could persuade friendly troops that they were under attack from a new direction. Cobra crews, therefore, made gun runs parallel to the frontlines.

LAM SON 719

By December 1970 the North Vietnamese had infiltrated 18,000 more troops and 20 AAA battalions into Laos and Cambodia. AAA guns ranging from 12.7mm to 100mm in size were in 3,000 prepared sites in the Laotian panhandle, many having been transported to the southeast of Tchepone. In response to this build up, US and South Vietnamese strategists planned an airborne operation codenamed *Lam Son 719* aimed at cutting off the Ho Chi Minh Trail and seizing NVA Base Area 604 near Tchepone. The ARVN force, totaling 34 battalions, would then destroy Trail convoys and attack major Base Area 611, before returning to South Vietnam via the A Shau Valley after engaging yet more convoys.

This PT-76 was one of a handful knocked out at Ben Het in March 1969 when five NVA battalions assaulted the Special Forces camp there and another at Dak To. The PT-76 light amphibious tank was developed for the Soviet Army to make river crossings in Europe. Although more vulnerable to air attack than the T-54, it often broke through ARVN defenses in confrontations such as the Dak To assault. (US Army)

This massive ARVN airborne operation launched on February 8, 1971 marked the first appearance in quantity of North Vietnamese armored divisions, which made coordinated tank and infantry assaults. Intended to boost ARVN morale and frustrate North Vietnamese invasion plans, *Lam Son 719* achieved neither aim and severely tested the whole airborne concept. It also proved the necessity of Cobra gunships. As the 101st Aviation Battalion's *Lam Son 719* post-mortem stated, "In the early stages it became apparent that the armed helicopter was vital to the successful accomplishment of the airmobile mission." While enemy AAA increased, the proportion of gunships to lift helicopters rose from two gunships for 20 UH-1H "slicks" to two gunships per five UH-1Hs. "This created a major control and allocation problem," with massive combat hours flown by limited numbers of Cobras.

US support came mainly from the 101st Airborne Division (Mobile), which, along with ARVN units, provided 700 lift and gunship helicopters. More than 2,000 tactical aircraft from USAF, US Marine Corps, and US Navy squadrons were available, with additional support from US artillery units and engineers. However, neither US advisors nor TACAIR units were substantially involved in the planning. A diversionary US operation, *Dewey Canyon II*, on January 22, 1971 secured the western part of Quang Tri Province and re-occupied the abandoned US Marine Corps base at Khe Sanh as the forward operating base for the helicopter force. The 101st Airborne Division provided two ARA batteries of AH-1Gs for "general support," including LZ preparation or engaging targets of opportunity, specifically armored vehicles and AAA.

OPPOSITE BOTTOM
AH-1G 67-15591 *GRIM REAPER* served a full tour with C Troop, 3/17th Cavalry from July 1968 until it was destroyed on August 9, 1970. The nickname was also applied to a UH-1C gunship of the 189th AHC in 1969. (US Army)

In 1971 D Company, 101st Airborne Division was based at both the Lang Vei Special Forces Camp (seen here) and at Phu Bai. The 101st had received its first Cobras in December 1968, and they were heavily involved in *Lam Son 719*. The unit had strict criteria regarding claims for damaged or destroyed tanks, stating that "To classify a tank destroyed, the tank must explode or burn. For it to be classified as immobilized, parts have to be seen to have been blown off and the tank incapable of further movement without repair." (Terry Panopalis collection)

US Intelligence staff were still skeptical about NVA armor entering the conflict, but two 361st AWC AH-1Gs – the first Cobra unit in the II Corps area – attacked a pair of tanks in Kontum province near Base Area 609. Four more were detected under trees and others were seen on January 30, again by the 361st.

Shortly after *Lam Son 719* commenced on February 8, seven UH-1s were quickly shot down. Cobra crews were summoned by the 21st Ranger Battalion to attack three tanks and an artillery tractor on Route 9 two days later – low cloud had precluded tactical air support. They fired rockets, but no tanks were claimed. Cobras encountered 12.7mm machine gun fire as they "prepped" LZ *Delta*, one of the first landing zones on the ARVN's westward route. An OH-6A and AH-1G 68-17106 were shot down, but the crews were recovered. Further along Route 9 was Aluoi, where five truck-mounted 12.7mm guns were preventing helicopter landings. Like the next LZ, closely surrounded by 12.7mm emplacements, it required the attention of Cobras.

There was a surge of PT-76 and T-34 tanks into the area from February 28, and 15 were eliminated from the air. Most were static and heavily camouflaged, with some hidden inside huts. Nevertheless, they were visible to AC-130 gunships' infra-red "eyes." Others were spotted by low-flying Cobra scouts, yielding targets for TACAIR.

The ARVN armored column advanced slowly along Route 9, having received orders directly from President Thieu to avoid over-aggressive engagements. This gave the NVA time to transfer in more artillery and AAA to flank Route 9 and surround potential LZs. Six sites were approached by airborne forces on March 3 to establish artillery Fire Support Bases (FSBs), and at one code-named *Lolo* 11 out of 20 UH-1s and two Cobras were destroyed by well-prepared AAA. A further 35 helicopters were heavily damaged. Other sites were more thoroughly "prepped" by Cobras and air strikes, prompting the NVA to move closer with camouflaged AAA.

On February 20, FSB 31, north of Route 9, was targeted by 20 PT-76 and T-54 tanks, supported by 2,000 infantrymen. Intense AAA made Cobra attacks too hazardous, but 11 tanks were destroyed by TACAIR and artillery. An ARVN tank column attempting relief of FSB 31 was delayed and instead engaged North

Vietnamese tanks in the first major armor-versus-armor confrontation of the war. More T-54s climbed the hills to FSBs 30 and 31. Tactical jets, B-52s, and Cobras (between the air strikes) knocked out PT-76s and T-34s, but dreadful weather prevented sustained air attacks and the remaining NVA tanks broke through the FSBs' defenses. Some ARVN troops had M72 LAWs but lacked training in their use, so the missiles they fired simply bounced off the tanks' sloping fronts. Nevertheless, 21 NVA tanks were reportedly destroyed and 1,500 soldiers killed.

FSBs 30 and 31 again faced determined NVA armored attacks from March 1, when 15 tanks were destroyed with bombs and rockets. Although an AC-130 Spectre and 36 tactical fighter sorties maintained ten hours of pressure on the enemy from March 2, more FSBs were surrounded and overrun, leading to the emergency recovery of ARVN troops under heavy fire. Evacuation by helicopter often required two hours of AAA suppression before Hueys could approach. Four Cobras or UH-1Cs also escorted helicopters trying to resupply the embattled FSBs and evacuate casualties. Fighters armed with 500lb Mk 82 general purpose (GP) bombs or BLU-27 napalm canisters would fly up to 15 sorties suppressing AAA ahead of a landing, with the helicopters' flightpath being obscured by CBU-12 smoke screen bombs.

Although Cobra units were inadequately equipped to deal with tanks in *Lam Son 719*, six were destroyed and eight immobilized out of the 66 sighted by AH-1G crews. Tactics used by 2/17th Air Cavalry crews involved firing flechettes at extreme range to eliminate the tanks' accompanying infantry, following through with high-explosive or white phosphorous 2.75in. rockets and gunfire before calling in fighter-bombers. Mk 5 HEAT rockets were in short supply, and the 2.75in. weapons were only effective against thin-skinned PT-76s. Launching them inevitably took the Cobra crews within range of 12.7mm guns. The Picatinny Arsenal in New Jersey responded with the manufacture of 1,000 improved M247 HEDP warheads in just four days. These gave HEAT rockets a longer range, thus keeping Cobra crews away from the worst of the AAA. They were delivered to the AH-1G base at Lai Khe from April 15.

Flechettes not only devastated infantry supporting the tanks, they could force tank crews to close their hatches and abandon their turret-mounted 12.7mm guns. White phosphorous rockets sometimes detonated their auxiliary external fuel tanks. Well placed 20mm rounds could damage tank tracks, with eight T-54s being disabled in this way in addition to the six examples destroyed by Cobras. However, the uncertain accuracy of rocket fire, particularly under heavy AAA, often left AH-1G pilots with insufficient rounds to disable more than two tanks per sortie.

When TACAIR was summoned to bomb tanks identified by Cobras there were inevitable delays while jets flew from bases in Thailand and South Vietnam. Bad weather and increasing AAA limited both them and Cobras in their anti-armor efforts. FACs from the 834th Air Division at Tan Son Nhut AB handled complex scheduling, with new TACAIR flights arriving every ten minutes. Cobras then picked off the remaining defenses, but losses still occurred at sites such as *Lolo*, where 16 more Hueys were lost even after thorough "prepping."

At night, the attack role passed to USAF AC-130 and AC-119 gunships, which claimed 24 PT-76 tanks and other vehicles, adding to a total of 1,539 supply and troop-carrying vehicles, truck-mounted AAA and rocket launchers knocked out. Large quantities of supplies were also destroyed, particularly by *Arc Light* B-52s. In one such

mission on March 7, a cache of 1,220 122mm rockets was detonated. Artillery also contributed to stemming armored advances whenever it was in range, using coordinates provided by FACs or Cobras. Eight more tanks were knocked out by 155mm and 175mm guns on March 7–8. As COMUSMACV Gen Creighton W. Abrams commented, "He [the NVA] is losing tanks like he didn't care

Scout and armed reconnaissance missions and most sorties flown from the spring of 1972 required some low altitude flying by Cobra pilots. Passing over a typical Vietnamese village, the crew of *PATRICIA ANN* of C Troop, 7/1st Cavalry watch for signs of enemy activity among the huts. (US Army)

about having any more," but still they came. A 2/17th Air Cavalry Cobra crew saw 21 PT-76s approaching on March 19.

Shortly after *Lam Son 719* commenced, President Thieu decided to limit its scope to an attack on Tchepone in order to seize war materiel. On March 6, the ARVN's 1st Infantry Division was airlifted to the less defended LZ *Hope* near Tchepone in 120 Hueys, with 20 gunships escorting them, and only one UH-1 was lost. It was the largest helicopter airlift ever performed. Preparatory *Arc Light*s caused more than 2,000 secondary explosions. The main ARVN armored force then withdrew, but when its tank column stalled under heavy NVA attack, further enemy artillery and armor appeared despite punitive air attacks on their supply routes. On March 10 ten NVA tanks were destroyed in air attacks, but 20 others pursued the retreating ARVN column as it suffered breakdowns and artillery hits.

Standard Cobra tactics, requiring two aircraft to fly a racetrack over the LZ at 500–1,000ft, firing at any opposition, had to be revised for *Lam Son 719*. Assault helicopters entered the LZ at 30-second intervals at low altitude. Air Cavalry Cobras formed reconnaissance teams consisting only of AH-1Gs. One scout Cobra patrolled at low altitude, with three at higher levels ready to dive on any targets identified by the low Cobra or a "C&C" UH-1H at high altitude. Pilots, most of whom were not IFR qualified, had to manage poor visibility and uncertain communications, the latter caused partly by 1,500 captured ARVN radio sets that the NVA used to distract aircrew. The sheer weight of carefully positioned AAA fire made an assault force's normal 1,500ft approach altitude to LZs almost suicidal. Helicopters had to use "nap of the earth" approaches instead, with smaller groups converging on LZs from various directions.

The overall performance of the UH-1C during the operation was questioned in the 101st Airborne Division's report on *Lam Son 719*:

The major shortfall in aviation support was in the gunship category. The UH-1C gunship was not capable of performing adequately in the *Lam Son* environment. Performance limitations and the hostile anti-aircraft environment encountered limited the effectiveness of the 60 UH-1C aircraft assigned. The [AH-1Gs of the] 235th AWC [were] added to the task organization to compensate for the ineffectiveness of the UH-1C. Without the armed helicopter there could be no airmobile operations. The armed helicopter provides a capability for responsive, continuous, accurate close fire support offered by no other weapon within the US inventory.

Although the Cobra units' role in this controversial operation was described by the US Army Aviation Digest as "the best contemporary example of the AH-1 Cobra contesting enemy armor in combat", the 101st Airborne Division's report observed that:

The army needs tank-defeating armed helicopters. Had the [101st] Division entered *Lam Son 719* with a helicopter armed with an accurate, lethal, relatively long-range anti-tank weapon, it would have destroyed many more NVA tanks and would have rendered more effective close support to ARVN ground forces.

Ironically, it would be the UH-1B (in NUH-1B form), the first Huey gunship, that fired the first examples of such a weapon – the M26 TOW missile – in Vietnam, and then only in tiny numbers.

Gunships and TACAIR had at least prevented the ARVN force from isolation and destruction, but at a heavy cost. More than 1,100 elite ARVN troops were killed. The 8,000 TACAIR sorties flown accounted for 4,136 NVA dead. Seventy-four NVA tanks were destroyed and 144 tanks and APCs abandoned. Of the 117 Cobras involved, 101 were hit but only 16 were lost. A total of 105 helicopters (14 percent) were lost altogether, and 68 percent received moderate or severe damage. Of those, at least 120 were not expected to return to service.

QUANG TRI

In November 1971 Cobras from A Troop, 7/17th Air Cavalry had assisted the ARVN's 11th and 23rd Ranger Battalions and 45th Infantry Division in Cambodia, where they discovered vast quantities of enemy weapons and supplies. Despite these finds, the magnitude of the NVA's 1972 Easter Offensive launched four months later was still unexpected.

As previously noted in this volume, the vast majority of the anti-armor clashes involving Cobras occurred during North Vietnam's *Nguyen Hue* invasion of South Vietnam. This was because tanks, supported by infantry, spearheaded assaults on ARVN forces in the I Corps area. Boldly moving in daylight across open country that favored such warfare, 260 tanks of the NVA's 202nd and 203rd Armored Regiments rolled over numerous ARVN FSBs from April 2. The ARVN's 20th Tank Squadron with M48A3s responded, destroying six tanks on the 2nd, followed by a further 16 T-54s on April 9.

However, many ARVN troops were panicked by tanks, and it was left mainly to TACAIR and Cobras to stall the advance of massive NVA forces. The 20th Tank

Regiment had lost all of its M48A3s by the end of April, and Quang Tri, the first South Vietnamese provincial capital to be lost, was occupied by NVA troops on May 2. As the population was evacuated along Highway 1, NVA forces shelled refugee columns, killing more than 2,000 civilians.

LOC NINH

On March 30, as part of the Easter Offensive, the NVA's 9th Infantry Division, led by 100 T-54, PT-76, and Type 59 tanks of the 202nd and 203rd Armored Regiments, entered Military Region III in South Vietnam from Cambodia, confronting the ARVN's 1st Armored Cavalry Brigade. The NVA's 5th Infantry Division, with 10,000 men, supported by the 26th Artillery Division, overran 20 FSBs and Camp Carroll near Loc Ninh on Route 13 in Binh Long Province. The invading troops seized artillery pieces and armored vehicles (some 460 of which were in the area) as they flooded into Military Region III.

ARVN forces eventually established a small tactical operations center (TOC) in Japanese-built bunkers near the airstrip at Loc Ninh, a small town in the French Cexco rubber plantation near Highway 13. The TOC was just 62 miles from Saigon. At 0300 hrs on April 5, two NVA regiments supported by 25 tanks followed up massive artillery barrages with an attack on the airstrip. A tank leading troops toward the TOC was destroyed by an AC-130, a second one was taken out by TACAIR bombs and napalm and a third by an M40 105mm recoilless rifle – a weapon for which the resident ARVN 9th Infantry Regiment had only six rounds! As the NVA continued to penetrate the airstrip's defenses, an M72 LAW bounced off a tank but its engine was disabled by AC-130 gunfire.

Six AH-1Gs and three OH-6As of F Troop, 9th Cavalry responded to the desperate call from the US advisors helping man the TOC. "Loc Ninh is under tank and heavy infantry attack. Any aircraft with armament please respond." USAF F-4 Phantom II units, A-37B Dragonflies from Bien Hoa's 8th Special Operations Squadron (SOS),

A shark-mouthed Cobra and accompanying "Loach" at a primitive forward base in February 1971. The AH-1G's ammunition doors (open in this view) could be lowered for emergency rescue. Two "passengers" could lie on the doors, linking arms through the space between. Pilots occasionally had to sleep on the doors. (Terry Panopalis collection)

TACAIR from Carrier Air Wing 9, embarked in the aircraft carrier USS *Constellation* (CVA-64), and VNAF fighter squadrons all headed for Loc Ninh. There was intense gunfire from hundreds of NVA troops surrounding the small ARVN enclave, much of it from captured 0.50-cal. machine guns.

The Cobras arrived quickly, and one, flown by CW2 Thomas Jones and Capt Donald Gooch, fired an entire rocket load into huge infantry formations. Capt Ron Timberlake's Cobra knocked out a PT-76 tank with 17lb warheads in a very low altitude rocket run, his AH-1G probably being saved from the lacerating groundfire by a flight of F-4 Phantom IIs that bombed the highway close to the helicopter's low-level attack run, distracting or killing many enemy soldiers.

A two-ship 2nd Battalion, 20th ARA Cobra flight led by CW3 Charles Windeler, with gunner Capt Hank Spengler (ex-101st Airborne Division), as "Max 34" (67-15594) was diverted to the battle following radio reports of armor and heavy AAA. 20th ARA crews had only previously experienced 12.7mm gunfire. Two more Cobras, flown by CW3 Barry McIntyre and Capt William Leach, joined them over Loc Ninh to neutralize an AAA site in tree cover. As a "heavy fire" team, they had the unit's typical load of high-explosive rockets inboard and flechettes on outboard pylons.

Windeler led a rocket run and Spengler fired 40mm grenades, pulling out of a 45-degree dive at 3,000ft to avoid AAA. They lined up for a second attack, with deadly 12.7mm fire now streaming toward them, and they were hit at 300ft. The engine exploded and the controls burned out, forcing Windeler to turn toward a clearing and seek a landing area. However, the tail boom quickly burned through and fell off, the rotor separated and the helicopter spun to the left and crashed. There were no survivors.

At Loc Ninh, 57mm AAA appeared, and one site was taken out by an F Troop, 9th Cavalry Cobra with flechettes on April 6, followed shortly thereafter by a 12.7mm gun hidden in the villa of a plantation owner. Heavy cloud cover favored the NVA attackers, but it also provided limited cover for Cobras as they dived through holes in the undercast, firing at troops and vehicles in conditions that would normally have grounded them.

Another tank from a force of 30 T-54s, Type 63s, and ZSU-57-2 SPAAGs lumbered toward the TOC on April 7, its crew determined to capture the US advisors. Typically for such operations at Loc Ninh, the tank commanders appeared to work independently without direct infantry support. Above the tank flew an OH-6A, finding targets for Cobras of the 79th AFA and D/229th AHB. Its driver was distracted by the "Loach," and his tank was hit by an M72 LAW fired by Capt Mark A. Smith, who had effectively taken command of the defense of the ARVN area on the ground, organizing air strikes

Photographed after the Loc Ninh engagement with NVA armor on April 5, 1972, F Troop, 9th Cavalry pilots Capt Ron Timberlake, WO1 Bob Stein and Lt Parks (Blue Platoon leader) are seen with "Cav" headgear beside a "Hunter" AH-1G. (US Army)

Capt Mark A. Smith, MACVs heroic advisor at Loc Ninh and organizer of its defenses. Wounded and captured in that losing battle, he subsequently returned to the US Army following his release in February 1973 and eventually retired in 1985 as a major after commanding the US Army Special Forces Detachment in South Korea. (US Army)

despite being wounded several times. Cobra support could be managed directly from the TOC, while other air activity was the responsibility of FAC pilots.

Further tank advances occurred that same day when TACAIR sorties were paused while a diverted *Arc Light* was called in. Unfortunately, the ARVN general controlling the B-52s gave crews target coordinates two miles from Loc Ninh. During the 30 minutes enforced lull while the air strikes were carried out, NVA forces seized their opportunity and invaded the TOC. A T-54 and a Type 63 were destroyed when TACAIR was resumed, but by then only 80 ARVN troops remained to defend the airstrip.

F Troop, 9th Cavalry OH-6A pilot 1Lt Richard Dey planned to rescue the besieged US advisors, although Capt Smith refused to leave. Dey suggested dropping gas grenades on the TOC to incapacitate the NVA troops, allowing him to swoop in and grab the Americans. His scout was driven off by 12.7mm fire, however. ARVN survivors soon surrendered, but four American advisors, including Capt Smith, fought on until they were captured on April 8. Three more advisors had escaped to the nearby Cat Lo bridge, where a D/229th AHB "Pink" team led by Capt John Whitehead's "Loach" went to rescue them. Flying through heavy 12.7mm AAA, they eventually collected the Americans and four ARVN survivors. The tiny helicopter had to take off with nine aboard, and several troops hanging on to the skids were picked off by 12.7mm fire.

The NVA's success had cost them numerous armored vehicles and 7,000 troops, many of them to Cobra attacks. For the ARVN, it was a salutary lesson in underestimating NVA capability and determination.

AN LOC

In the wake of the Easter Offensive, ARVN Task Force (TF) 52 had attempted to withdraw to the provincial capital of An Loc, but it was ambushed by NVA elements that were in turn attacked by two Cobras, inflicting heavy casualties. When TF 52's US advisors were wounded, a medevac UH-1H escorted by AH-1Gs tried to extract them. The Huey was driven off three times by enemy fire. On April 8, after all-night attacks by A-37Bs, two "Loaches" with four Cobra escorts made a new rescue effort. They were supported by a group of 79th AFA AH-1Gs that had flown in from Lai Khe, 40 miles south of An Loc. Immediately upon landing, the OH-6As were swamped by ARVN troops attempting to escape, and both had to retreat after suffering heavy damage.

The following day, as a prelude to the sustained Battle of An Loc, an unusually large "heavy team" of five F Troop, 9th Cavalry Cobras hit an NVA regimental headquarters in a village southwest of the town. Attacking through extensive cloud cover while the lead AH-1G remained above it, the helicopters were hard to see as they dived steeply, starting numerous fires. Two days later, on April 11, F Troop, 9th Cavalry Cobras hit a tank with 17lb warheads after it was spotted by a "Loach" crew.

The previous day, Bien Hoa's 229th AHB, with Cobra escorts, had lifted two battalions from the ARVN's 8th Infantry Regiment battalions into An Loc after Highway 13 was cut off by NVA forces. The latter had quickly set up ZSU-2 twin-barrel AAA guns and 37mm batteries to defeat helicopters trying to bolster the defense of An Loc. Four ARVN M48s made a disastrous attempt to clear the road, blundering into NVA forces that quickly swamped them and their fuel trucks – the latter were set on fire.

Heavy shelling had started to destroy An Loc by April 12, forcing the 5th Division commander, Gen Le Van Hung, and his US advisory team to move their headquarters to an underground, Japanese-built complex made of steel-reinforced concrete. Tanks, which had been sighted by ARVN 3rd Ranger Group patrols the previous day, were heard advancing through the Michelin rubber plantations surrounding the town. They were initially targeted by USAF AC-130 Spectre gunships and two fighters. At 0515 hrs on April 13, 15 NVA tanks and soldiers from the 9th Infantry Division attacked An Loc's local airstrip at Dong Long, detonating major ammunition and fuel stores. By then a hilltop FSB had been taken, and its artillery was re-focused on An Loc. An F Troop, 9th Cavalry Cobra subsequently fired a full load of rockets at the NVA gunners manning the site.

While T-54Bs occupied the airstrip, others advanced down Highway 13, flanked by infantry. One tank and some supply trucks were soon destroyed by a Spectre, while a B-52 strike detonated a large NVA ammunition dump. The remaining NVA tanks pressed on regardless, and a second hilltop FSB was overrun. Its surviving occupants retreated into An Loc, leaving behind an ideal location for NVA AAA batteries. More tanks approached from the north, east, and west, while artillery focused on the town center.

Two of the T-54Bs broke through the 3rd Ranger Group's defenses on the northern perimeter of An Loc, advancing down Highway 13. ARVN troops, many of whom had never seen tanks, panicked, just as the NVA had intended. However, they soon saw that there was a lack of coordination between enemy troops and armor. When the NVA soldiers were neutralized by 81mm mortar rounds and gunfire and a T-54B was hit by a 105mm shell, the remaining tanks either stopped or continued on alone without infantry support. They quickly became targets for the defenders' plentiful supplies of hand-launched M72 LAWs or circling Cobras.

Eventually, the T-54Bs re-grouped and continued their advance into An Loc along Ngo Quyen Street. Crews drove with hatches open, expecting the citizens to welcome them despite the artillery devastation already

Troops from the 8th Infantry Regiment celebrate the demise of a T-54B from the 20th Armored Brigade in An Loc on June 3, 1972. It was destroyed by rockets from an AH-1G, and the smoke grenade that the soldiers detonated on its surface indicated to other Cobras or TACAIR that the tank has already been disabled. (AP/Alamy)

inflicted on the city. Some had even brought fresh uniforms for the anticipated victory celebration. From high buildings, ARVN soldiers and armed citizens fired down on them killing numerous tank crew. As they pressed on, the third tank was stopped by an M72 LAW and its occupants were shot as they leapt out. The column stalled, ARVN troops gained confidence and three more tanks were incapacitated by M72 LAWs.

Nevertheless, the first two tanks drove on, heading for the 5th Division's HQ bunker. An informer had apparently told the enemy its location, and it seemed that Gen Hung and the American advisors were doomed. The general had a grenade ready for a suicidal gesture, but as the tank turned to fire at the HQ bunker, Col Le Nguyen Vy stepped out of it and fired an M72 LAW that caused the tank's engine to erupt in flames. Other 7th Regiment troops sealed its fate. When the one remaining tank turned to leave, it was hit by 105mm artillery and finished off by the 8th Reconnaissance Company. By the time the last T-54B had been knocked out it was 0900 hrs.

Loaded with 27 rockets each, two AH-1G Cobras of F Battery, 79th AFA had taken off ("skids up") just after dawn and headed directly to An Loc, where they provided continuous support to the embattled ARVN. "Heavy Pink" teams became standard during the battle for the town, with a "Loach" at low level, a Cobra at 1,500ft, and a second gunship at 2,500ft, both ready to dive and fire instantly. The lower Cobra responded first with grenades and gunfire, while the high helicopter set up for its rocket pass. In a variation of this tactic, the "Purple" team had a "Loach" and two Cobras all approaching at low altitude, taking advantage of cloud cover, and a "C&C" UH-1H above.

The senior US advisor at An Loc at the time was Col William H. Miller, on his third Vietnam tour. He warned AH-1Gs from F Battery, 79th AFA to stay away from the town due to intense enemy AAA, believing that their rockets would have little impact on the tanks. However, Cobra leader Maj Larry McKay, F Battery commander and gunner for CW2 Barry McIntyre in AH-1G "Serpent 6", advised him that his helicopters had HEAT in their outboard pods. Miller, who later wrote he wished he had had "Stukas" available to hit the tanks, let McKay and the second helicopter (flown by Capt Billy Causey, with gunner 1Lt Steve Shields) try.

McKay duly asked troops of the 8th Reconnaissance Company to use smoke grenades to mark the tanks that had already been knocked out. The first tank victim for an AH-1G in this phase of the invasion was among six T-54Bs entering the town. Advancing down a fairly narrow road, quite close together with their turrets open and machine gunners standing, they were driving ahead of their infantry, operating as a separate force. Miller asked for minimal collateral damage to An Loc's citizenry, as he thought the "Serpents'" 152 rockets

Tank killer Maj Larry McKay, commander of F Battery, 79th AFA, played a key role in halting T-54Bs that were advancing into An Loc on April 13, 1972. (US Army)

would have standard 17lb warheads. In fact, HEAT rockets were designed to penetrate a small area of armor and then explode inside the tank. McIntyre also had 17lb rockets inboard.

To focus the attack, McIntyre flew a "wingover" and dived at an angle of around 35 degrees from 5,000ft, firing several HEAT rockets at the leading tank's engine compartment at relatively close range and pulling out at around 3,000ft. The explosion blew the turret off and caused a conflagration from exploding shells. AAA was minimal at the time, and the Cobra crews then took out another tank among the leading vehicles and also the last tank, trapping the rest of the group which was part of a 40-strong armored assault on the city. Another, T-54, "954," was destroyed later in the day using a 17lb warhead, and a tank in the 3rd Ranger Group's area was knocked out by an F-4 Phantom II. In total, F Battery, 79th AFA destroyed five tanks that day, while Cobras from the 229th AHB rocketed 21 supply vehicles. AAA from 12.7mm, 23mm, and 37mm guns soon became intense.

A T-54 entering the town was wrecked by newly trained teenagers firing an M72 LAW from a second-story window. Another was lost to an identical weapon employed by a soldier from the 3rd Ranger Group and a third tank was abandoned by its crew (who were shot) after a hand grenade detonated its fuel tank. Fresh tank formations were quickly assembled outside the town, only to be destroyed by TACAIR. Those that continued to prowl through the streets of An Loc, whose center measured only 3,000ft x 4,500ft, became targets for Cobras, with some risk posed to ARVN and civilian personnel. The helicopter gunships eventually claimed 20 tanks destroyed in total, losing five Cobras and eight crew in the process. Col Miller commented, "The Cobras were the instruments of our salvation."

Once AH-1Gs and TACAIR were spotted overhead, soldiers from the NVA's 272nd Regiment abandoned their accompanying tanks. They then roamed the streets without clear direction, for many of the potential informers within An Loc had been quickly arrested. Tanks ran into ambushes, and their command structure (armor and infantry had separate commanders) broke down when Cobras decimated the infantry. One was destroyed by an ARVN 105mm round, bringing total confirmed tank losses for April 13 to 16. Many blocked the narrow streets with wreckage. Encouraged by the tank kills, Gen Hung assembled civilian anti-tank squads firing captured B40 and B41 RPGs or M72 LAWs. Troops also listened for enemy mortars firing, and told US advisors of their approximate launching position. FACs then called in Cobras to attack the mortar sites.

CW2 Ronald L. Tusi of F Battery, 79th AFA was awarded the Distinguished Service Cross (DSC) for his outstanding actions over An Loc on April 15. Staff in the 5th Division's HQ bunker saw more tanks heading for their position, firing at the entrance from around 500ft. They were too close to call in TACAIR, so

CW2 Ronald L. Tusi of F Battery, 79th AFA, 3rd Brigade, 1st Cavalry (center) and fellow Cobra flyers pose on an abandoned T-54. Tusi was a US Navy SEAL prior to joining the US Army. Awarded a DSC for his exploits over An Loc on April 15, 1972, he was killed on August 6, 1974 testing "Night Owl" night vision goggles when his helicopter hit power lines at low altitude. (US Army)

Cobras were requested. Four F/79th AFA AH-1Gs were loaded with HEAT and put on 30-minute standby to stage from their Bear Cat Base near Bien Hoa to Lai Khe. Having previously refueled and re-armed at the latter site, neither option was then available after the ammunition store at Lai Khe was hit by artillery shells. All AH-1G crews had to refuel at Bien Hoa until Lai Khe was back up and running on April 17.

By 0625 hrs five Cobras were over An Loc ready to engage armor a few yards from the 5th Division's HQ bunker. The 12.7mm AAA was by then extremely intense, but Tusi and Capt Billy Causey flew through it and fired HEAT rockets at the approaching tank column, knocking out four T-54s and PT-76s and severely damaging a fifth. The rest of the column turned away as Tusi remained over the battlefield until his ammunition was exhausted, forcing the infantry to retreat. He went on to claim ten tanks destroyed during his five Vietnam tours.

Extracts from a Third Regional Assistance Command (TRAC) journal for F Troop, 9th Cavalry and F Troop, 79th ARA Cobras on April 15 underline both their anti-armor role and the pace of operations from Bien Hoa:

> 0255 hrs – F/9 to stage from Lai Khe. Be prepared to depart Bien Hoa at 0700H and to engage enemy armored vehicles, conduct visual reconnaissance in designated boxes. F/79 to be on standby (30 min alert). Be prepared to engage enemy armored vehicles.
>
> 0520 hrs – Bounce Heavy Fire Team of F/79 with nails [flechettes]. Marginal weather for helicopters.
>
> 0625 hrs – F/79 has five ships at An Loc.
>
> 0815 hrs – TRAC requests F/9 to be bounced to work Visual Recon Boxes. May need MAX [Cobras] to engage ground-to-air fire.
>
> 0940 hrs – Tanks 500m from TOC. Cav Troop to be used to find anti-aircraft positions for FAC.
>
> 1035 hrs – Troop concentrations and 10 tanks in [recce] box at 735894.
>
> 1050 hrs – Reports no 23mm or 37mm fire east of An Loc [silenced by Cobras] but a great deal of 12.7mm fire.
>
> 1135 hrs – Get 400 HEAT rockets to Lai Khe asap.
>
> 1500 hrs – At 1450 hrs ten tanks were attacking An Loc. Nine were destroyed [including those by Tusi].

That same day, South Vietnamese reinforcements had attempted, and failed, to reach An Loc from the south. Two major assaults had been launched on the town on April 15, preceded by devastating artillery barrages that were rapidly reducing all of An Loc's buildings to rubble. More than 1,000 rounds were fired in 90 minutes from 0430 hrs, with the 5th Division HQ bunker again being the main target. Following in the wake of the dawn attack, columns of tanks and infantry entered the city from the north and west at 0900 hrs, with armor pushing back the ARVN's 8th Infantry Regiment and 3rd Ranger Battalion. Five tanks were destroyed in quick succession by M72 LAWs and captured B40s fired by the 36th Ranger Battalion, the 51st Artillery Battalion's sole 105mm gun, and a USAF fighter. By 1000 hrs the Cobras were heavily involved, inflicting a heavy toll on enemy troops along the northwestern front. Nevertheless, by the end of the day the enemy had occupied most of the northern half of the town, losing ten more tanks in the process.

Outside the city limits, the assembled NVA regiments were frequently attacked by *Arc Light*s, TACAIR, and AC-130s. The latter were particularly accurate in pinpoint attacks with 40mm and 105mm cannon on NVA mortar positions near ARVN lines. Closer to friendly troops, the Cobras, flying non-stop daily missions, or A-37Bs were preferable for pin-point attacks, although at considerable risk to the pilots.

Just one of the 300 6.1lb shells carried by this ZSU-57-2 could easily bring down a Cobra at a range of more than three miles. Usually, the SPAAG's gunsights were set for fast jets, so its shells burst ahead of helicopters. This example was destroyed at An Loc during the Easter Offensive. (USAF)

On April 16, Lt Col Gordon Weed, commander of the Bien Hoa-based 8th SOS (equipped with A-37Bs), responded to a call from Gen Hung's staff that a T-54 was firing at point-blank range into the 5th Division's HQ bunker. Only 40 ARVN troops were available to defend it. Braving extreme 12.7mm and 37mm AAA, Weed dropped a 250lb bomb directly on the tank, but it failed to explode. Even though the AAA had by now increased in ferocity, he turned back for another bomb-run, this time taking out the tank and killing many of its supporting troops. That same day, to the east, a Cobra hunter/killer team found and silenced 23mm and 37mm AAA sites, while other AH-1Gs fought back enemy forces at the northern edge of the town, enabling the ARVN's 8th Infantry Regiment to retake its positions. AAA and Strela SAMs were most active in the north.

A new tank assault by nine T-54s and two ZSU 57-2s SPAAGs on the 8th Infantry Regiment in the southwest of the city commenced immediately after artillery barrages on April 17. They had got to within 300ft of the 5th Division's HQ bunker when Cobras and ARVN infantry repelled them. The following day a T-54 stopped outside the town's Catholic church, where many citizens had sought refuge, and fired on it. When the tank ran out of ammunition its crew were killed, as were tankers who targeted Quoc Hoan school, killing many children.

Extra AAA emplacements had been moved closer to An Loc's boundaries on three sides by April 17, making the Cobra crews' mission tasking increasingly hazardous – 12.7mm and 23mm weapons were re-located on buildings in northern An Loc to fire at medevac, Cobras and re-supply helicopters.

The NVA's 271st Anti-Aircraft Regiment assembled in a plantation west of An Loc for a final, decisive assault. Trees provided complete top-cover from observation. However, it happened to be in a "kill-box" measuring three miles by a mile for a "tactical" *Arc Light* raid. Terrible casualties canceled the NVA attack. Tank incursions continued through to the end of April, including the threat of a 20-strong armored

ENGAGING THE ENEMY

An AH-1G gunner operated the M28A1 dual-weapon turret with a moveable pantographic compensating sight system, using information from an air data sensor and estimated range data via an electronic control sub-assembly (under his control panel) which had azimuth and elevation amplifiers and control circuits. Often, a gunner would aim by "walking" tracers to the target, rather than using the sight. Here, he is firing at an NVA Type 63 APC in a rubber plantation near An Loc in April 1972. The aircraft commander would follow up a gunnery pass with 2.75in. rockets. Rocket-firing Cobras were credited with ten T-54s and three PT-76s destroyed and six T-54s significantly damaged between March 30 and May 11, 1972.

formation approaching Lai Khe on the 24th and numerous tanks in An Loc two days later. An F Troop, 79th ARA Heavy Fire Team of Cobras with HEAT dealt with both attacks. *Arc Light* strikes also intensified. After one particular *Arc Light,* an NVA commander ordered his troops to shelter in the bomb craters. His orders were overheard by US radio monitors and a second *Arc Light* was diverted to the same map coordinates, wiping out most of the regiment. ARVN tanks from the 1/8th Company also knocked out three T-54s and scattered the rest.

In An Loc itself, ammunition soon began to run low, the final artillery pieces were destroyed and supply shortages increased. However, ARVN troops fought on, with many units showing greater determination than their US advisors had expected. USAF C-130s and C-123s dropped supplies from 600ft, although two-thirds of their parachute-delivered bundles fell in enemy-held areas. A 374th Tactical Airlift Wing C-130E was shot down on April 18 and a second fell to AAA during a night delivery one week later. The defenders

Murder Inc. was AH-1G 67-15649 of the 2/20th ARA, marked with the unit's distinctive "Blue Max" insignia on the "dog house." It is seen here in early 1971 with a "Heavy Hog" weapons load of four M159 launchers. The helicopter also has the wiring panels beneath the cockpit for the M35 20mm gun system. 67-15649 served with the 2/20th ARA until it was destroyed on May 11, 1972 during the defense of An Loc. (Terry Panopalis collection)

were reduced to using anti-tank mines made from 155mm shells, destroying two tanks with them. Four more were eliminated during a new, failed, assault from the north on April 19, but the city was now completely sealed off. Another incursion by two T-54s and two PT-76s was stopped with M72 LAWs on April 21, five more were removed by an AC-130 and three T-54s attacking the 5th Division's HQ without infantry support were all wrecked by M72 LAWs and Claymore mines.

When the third major assault finally began on May 5, ARVN defenders had been reduced from 7,500 to 4,000 men. By then, Col Miller, the US advisor who had valiantly sustained the ARVN defenders for a month, had been replaced by Col Walker Ulmer, flown in with Cobras escorting his Huey. A massive artillery barrage on May 11 was followed by columns of six to eight tanks approaching An Loc from all directions. Numerous *Arc Light* strikes were diverted to destroy much of the encroaching force, and six more tanks, mainly PT-76s, were taken out with M72 LAWs. Punitive air defenses accounted for an F Troop, 79th ARA Cobra, two 21st Tactical Air Support Squadron O-2A FAC aircraft (downed by SA-7s) and 1Lt Michael Blassie's 8th SOS A-37B, which was struck multiple times by 23mm fire during a napalm attack over the town's perimeter. Hundreds of aircraft were by then involved in trying to save An Loc. Six more tanks, including a BTR-50 amphibious APC, were destroyed as the enemy again advanced within a few yards of the 5th Division's HQ bunker.

The lost Cobra (68-15009) from F Troop, 79th ARA, flown by Capts Rodney L. Strobridge and back-seater Robert J. Williams (a former Cobra instructor), was hit by an SA-7 at 4,800ft on May 11. The helicopter was part of a "heavy fire team" three-Cobra escort for an early morning "Dust-Off" UH-1H collecting wounded ARVN soldiers from the edge a rubber plantation. The Cobras fired into the trees around the LZ, having already shot at two NVA armored vehicles at 1210 hrs. Forced down to altitudes below 3,000ft by heavy cloud, they were within range of both AAA and SA-7s.

Like other Cobra crews, Strobridge and Williams had received no training for dealing with SAMs. Suddenly, a white corkscrew smoke trail was seen darting from the plantation, heading for the Cobra and homing onto its exhaust. The helicopter's tail boom separated upon being hit, and it entered a flat spin, exploding at the edge of the clearing with the loss of both crew. The "Dust-Off" pilot reported, "One minute it was there and the next it was gone." Bodies were not recovered.

NVA tanks had been severely reduced, with 40 having been lost by May 11. Furthermore, battalions suffered heavy casualties, having their ranks reduced from 350 to 90 men on average. The TRAC journal of F Troop, 9th Cavalry for May 11 records the Cobras' strenuous day:

> 1420 hrs – tanks have been sighted at An Loc. Request Heavy Fire Team to be on station at 0600 hrs. Will have Lai Khe opened early.
>
> 0625 hrs – Tanks are inside the An Loc perimeter. Launch second Heavy Fire Team.
>
> 0640 hrs – There are 200 HEAT rockets at Lai Khe.
>
> 0805 hrs – A-37 shot down 2km north of An Loc. F/9 Cav heavy team covering downed pilot [Blassie].
>
> 1025 hrs – F/79 claims four tanks destroyed.
>
> 1740 hrs – An Loc update total 13 tanks destroyed today. Only one penetration by two tanks and NVA platoon.

The May 11 thrust was intended as the last major tank attack on the city. Four were knocked out by F Troop, 79th ARA and 11 by M72 LAWs-wielding troops and TACAIR. Cobras had eliminated 12 tanks and 25 transport vehicles in all, together with an estimated 1,040 NVA troops. Six more tanks had been immobilized with severe damage. The losses would have been even greater but for a pause in air strikes after Blassie was shot down. Although he had crashed close to enemy lines, a rescue was attempted. Blassie's death was confirmed in October. Poor weather delayed further air strikes, allowing enemy tanks to again threaten ARVN positions until a series of six *Arc Light*s stopped their progress, destroying several.

Only two AH-1Gs from the 229th AHB were available to deal with an early morning attack on An Loc from the south on May 12. They were directed against mortar positions in a plantation 900ft from ARVN lines, neutralizing the weapons and several other targets. By then tanks were appearing unpredictably in the town in small numbers, driving fast and charging through buildings to terrify the inhabitants. A brief night attack on May 13–14 was mounted predominantly by PT-76s, indicating that T-54 units were now suffering from a lack of tanks. An ARVN sergeant fired two M72 LAWs from a roof at a range of 30ft, detonating the ammunition stores of two PT-76s.

The following day Cobras escorted an SS-11 ground team to An Loc, but they could find no tank targets. However, AAA fire in the locality remained constant, with five more aircraft having been brought down by May 14. Although tactical aircraft were told to avoid An Loc, Cobra pilots were never refused permission to operate in that hostile environment.

The 229th AHB Cobra crew of Capts Roger Fox and Mike Henry, with OH-6A crew Capt John B. Whitehead and Sgt Raymond F. Waite, on their second mission of

May 15, approached An Loc from the south at 1,500 ft and saw a truck-mounted twin-23mm ZSU-2 that subsequently crumbled under the impact of four rockets. Whitehead then found a T-54 and Fox took out the 12.7mm turret gunner with flechettes. They also fired their remaining standard 2.75in. rockets at it, with little effect. The tank was finally destroyed by a 105mm shell fired by an orbiting AC-130.

Despite orders from Hanoi to continue attempts to seize An Loc, the incessant aerial bombardment and stout resistance by ARVN soldiers made another assault impossible. Some evacuees were allowed to leave the town with Cobra escort, although many, including a large group of Buddhist monks, were machine-gunned by NVA troops on Highway 13.

A final thrust, planned for May 19, was abandoned after an *Arc Light* wiped out more than half the troops assembled for it. A tank formation attempted an attack from the south, but ARVN paratroopers swarmed the lone T-54, PT-76s and captured M113 APCs, dropping grenades through their hatches. Gradually, the NVA withdrew from An Loc, allowing it to be liberated on June 12. President Thieu's entourage visited the town by helicopter on July 7, escorted by AH-1Gs. Cobras had been active throughout the siege, with the AH-1Gs of the 229th AHB, 1st Cavalry Division alone having flown 13,000 sorties in April–May 1972 during the 93-day siege of An Loc. As Lt Col James H. Willbanks, a US advisor at An Loc, put it, "Cobras offered the difference between victory and defeat."

STRELA

The arrival of the 9K32 Strela (NATO reporting name SA-7 "Grail") forced major changes in helicopter and tactical air operations from May 1972. The weapon, which according to Cobra crews had first been used in-theater in June 1970, required a loader and a gunner, with the latter keeping the target in his sights for at least seven

A Soviet SA-7 gunner demonstrates the shoulder-launched missile, which by June 1972 made 7,000ft minimum altitudes essential for fixed-wing aircraft operating over South Vietnam. The Cobra's engine and hydraulics doors had extra insulation in an attempt to hide the helicopter's heat signature from the Strela's infra-red seeker head. (Public Domain)

seconds before firing. A Cobra's maximum effective altitude was 6,000ft, and SA-7s were thought to be capable of reaching 10,000ft at supersonic speed.

In mid-April 1972, a Cobra hunter/killer team leader reported being fired at by a missile near An Loc, the weapon leaving a white corkscrew smoke trail in its wake. He fired 17lb warheads at the launch site but his reported sighting was dismissed by Military Intelligence. Another SA-7 was seen near the DMZ on April 29, and a third was reported by an F Troop, 9th Cavalry Cobra pilot at 2,000ft over An Loc on May 8 – beyond the range of a B40 RPG, which was the presumed type of weapon involved. More were sighted on May 10, one of which damaged a Cobra's hydraulics.

After SA-7s caused confirmed losses on May 11, low-altitude attacks by VNAF A-37B Dragonflies were curtailed and AC-130 Spectre gunship operations were limited after a near loss over An Loc on May 12. Cobras reduced their exposure temporarily while TACAIR destroyed established ground-to-air missile sites, although these were for Chinese HQ-1 Red Flag (reverse-engineered SA-2) weapons directed at fixed-wing aircraft. Being man-portable, SA-7s had no set launch sites.

With most Cobra crews firing their rockets from 3,000ft at 218mph, they were at risk of being hit by a Strela. Advice to "go low" or stay above 7,000ft would have denied them attack roles. However, some missions were reallocated to AAA targets on Highway 13. Guns were often located in villages, requiring the accuracy provided by Cobras when it came to knocking them out. Following a significant increase in AAA around An Loc, a few crews resorted to firing rockets at extreme range, risking injury to friendly troops.

On May 24, F Troop, 9th Cavalry AH-1G 67-15836, crewed by CW2s John R. Henn and pilot Isaac Yoshiro Hosaka, was on a three-ship "Dust-off" escort from Lai Khe forward base when it was hit by a Strela near An Loc at 4,800ft. The helicopter immediately broke in half, spinning down behind enemy lines in flames and killing the crew, whose bodies were unrecoverable. An SA-7 hit the exhaust of F Troop, 9th Cavalry AH-1G 67-15718 at 1,500ft over An Loc at 0800 hrs on June 20, with 1Lt Louis K. Breuer and CW2 Burdette D. Townsend being killed when it crashed moments later. Along with wingman CW2 Andy Kisela, they had taken off from the 229th AHB's forward base near Tan Khai to cover the extraction of ARVN airborne troops from an ambush on Highway 13. Also flying on that mission were Lt Stephen Shields and West Point graduate Capt Ed Northrup in F Battery, 79th AFA AH-1G 67-15670 and two "Loaches."

Although the SA-7 quickly became a potent threat to Cobra operations around An Loc, the innumerable AAA weapons (particularly 12.7mm guns) surrounding the town still accounted for most casualties. Just 20 minutes after Breuer and Townsend fell to a Strela, Northrup and Shields were caught between triangulated 12.7mm gun positions near An Loc as they fired rockets into a treeline. Crash-landing, they dashed to a bomb crater for refuge from NVA troops patrolling nearby. A gunfight ensued in which both men, armed only with 0.38-cal. side-arms, were killed by gunners manning dug-in 12.7mm weapons as they dashed toward another treeline. Their deaths meant that eight of F Troop, 9th Cavalry's 32 aircrew had been lost in action defending An Loc.

An SA-7 destroyed the AH-1G of Capts Mike Brown and Marco Cordon the following day (June 21) six miles south of An Loc. They were part of A Battery, F/79th AFA's "Chalk" flight – a heavy fire team escorting the ARVN troop extraction around an LZ near Highway 13. Flight leader CW2 Ron Tusi, with Capt Harry Davis, in "Serpent 12" orbited the site at low altitude while Brown and Cordon, with CW3 Russ Toms and WO Ron McCullough in the second Cobra, fired rockets and grenades into NVA mortar positions from above 4,000ft.

Suddenly, Brown received a "Missile! Missile! Missile!" warning from Tusi, and he steered the Cobra into a diving turn toward the advancing Strela – a pre-planned evasion maneuver to disguise the helicopter's exhaust heat. Part-way through this turn the SA-7 struck their Cobra, 67-15725 "Chalk 3", severing the tail boom. Brown began an autorotation, with the cyclic control pulled fully aft to keep the nose up as the helicopter slowly rotated to the right. He attempted to jettison the remaining wing-mounted ordnance and asked Cordon to fire off any turret ammunition to balance the center of gravity, but the electrical systems had failed. The spin increased markedly, and Brown "pulled maximum pitch" on the collective control to increase the pitch of the main rotor blades and soften the impact as the AH-1G neared the ground.

Fortunately, there was no fire, even though the engine was still running after the helicopter had hit the ground. Both crewmen struggled out of the wreck and were spotted by Tusi and Davis. They were picked up 15 minutes after the crash-landing by a B/229th AHB UH-1H flown by WO1 William Wright. Although the UH-1H was already overloaded with nine ARVN casualties, Wright tried to chop his way through tree-tops with his rotor to reach the crash site as NVA troops closed to within 600ft. As he approached, Brown and Cordon returned to their wrecked Cobra, climbed on top of it, grabbed the skids of Wright's Huey and were pulled aboard by the crew chief.

Meanwhile, Tusi and Davis had jettisoned their rocket pods, landed nearby, and dashed to the crash to find Brown and Cordon in the hope of airlifting them out on their Cobra's open ammunition doors. However, as they neared the wrecked AH-1G they saw the Huey take off safely with their squadronmates aboard, despite its tree-damaged rotor, so they ran back to their Cobra and returned to Lai Khe.

As these losses confirm, by June 1972 the Strela threat in South Vietnam had increased significantly. Slow-moving aircraft including helicopters were duly restricted to a hard deck altitude of 7,000ft. Between April 3 and November 15, 1972, 38 SA-7s were fired at US Army helicopters. Only four scored confirmed hits, three were the probable cause of losses and the remaining 31 missed either because of evasive maneuvers flown by helicopter pilots or weapon faults.

Following the sharp rise in Strela employment by the NVA, 79th ARA crews received a classified briefing on suggested survival tactics. They were told that upon spotting the SA-7's tell-tale corkscrew smoke trail they should immediately point the helicopter at it so that the weapon's infra-red seeker head could not detect the helicopter's 600°F exhaust heat. Crews were also shown a flare gun that was to be "fired out of the cockpit" if time permitted, distracting the seeker head. At that point the briefer was gently reminded that Cobra cockpit windows could not be opened in flight for this purpose.

It was several months before a realistic anti-missile device was available. The Bell "sugar scoop" (often dubbed the "toilet bowl") diverted exhaust gases upwards for dispersal by the rotor blades. Examples had been tested at Yuma for use in Europe-based helicopters and then placed in storage. Delivery to Vietnam took three months, with the Cobras of F Troop, 4th Cavalry being the first to be modified at Phu Bai in July 1972 – but only after the 'VIP' UH-1Hs used by senior US Army personnel had been equipped. Up to August 1972 a further 22 SA-7s were fired at helicopters with "sugar scoops" installed, without scoring hits.

KONTUM

After stalling at An Loc, the main NVA focus shifted on May 14 to taking Kontum and Pleiku in the third main thrust of the Easter Offensive. It was hoped that Kontum could be seized by May 18 (the date of the late President Ho Chi Minh's birthday), thus effectively cutting South Vietnam in two along Highway 19. As with An Loc, the plan was to infiltrate Kontum and use tanks and infantry to neutralize the ARVN/US command bunker. From there, troops would spread out into the town as they executed the "blossoming flower" tactic.

To facilitate Kontum's capture, the NVA's 7th Engineer Regiment constructed a road at night heading toward the town for use by tanks, with another built in the direction of Dak To. Although heavy attrition had decimated the NVA's T-54B ranks, some 50 examples led 50,000 troops in the assault on ARVN battalions at Tan Canh and Dak To, knocking out the dug-in ARVN M41 tanks with long-range AT-3 "Saggers" and dispersing troops, notwithstanding considerable US TACAIR opposition. Four T-54s of the 7th Tank Company destroyed ARVN emplacements on Dak To airfield despite Cobra pilot CW2 Pete Peterson twice firing rockets at them without inflicting any damage. As ARVN forces retreated in the direction of Kontum, they were covered by Cobras, 250 daily TACAIR strikes and *Arc Light*s, which were dropping ordnance costing $7million on a daily basis.

Nine US advisors at Dak To were rescued by the 57th AHC in Hueys, with a Cobra escort. ARVN forces, galvanized by the highly influential US advisor John Paul Vann, reorganized around the 23rd Infantry Division to defend Kontum. Vann had narrowly escaped from Tan Canh on April 24 when his personal OH-58 was rushed by ARVN troops who grabbed its skids on take-off, causing a crash. Two days later, a pair of AH-1Gs were captured intact on the ground by the NVA at the Dien Binh FSB on Route 14, 15 miles northwest of Kontum.

To help him with the impending defense of Kontum, Vann had secured 18 experimental M151A2 Jeep-mounted BGM-71/M26 TOW anti-tank missiles and two similarly armed *Hawk's Claw* NUH-1B Hueys, which were sent to Camp

This Chinese-built Type 63 light tank was photographed near the Ngo Mon Gate of the Thai Hoa Palace in Hue in 1972. Patriotic slogans decorate its flanks, but broken tracks indicate that its fighting days are over. (Alamy)

Holloway, in South Vietnam. The helicopters were subsequently escorted on all of their missions by two 7/17th Air Cavalry Cobras. Their first tank kill was a captured US M41A3 destroyed with a 50lb TOW missile on May 2 by CW2 Carrol Lain, together with three other NVA tanks.

Nevertheless, enemy artillery kept up its assault on Kontum, damaging two Cobras on the town's airfield. When the main North Vietnamese attack began on May 14, the two TOW helicopters, with Cobras, went into action at 0640 hrs and flew three sorties each. They destroyed five T-54s and four PT-76s with 21 missiles. TOWs, like "Sagger," needed a clear line of sight. On May 18 the NUH-1Bs destroyed another tank near the Krong Poko River and two ZSU-2 emplacements, while Cobras hit troops, vehicles, and artillery in open ground near Kontum.

The following day, a "human wave" NVA attack was repelled, largely by Cobras from Camp Holloway and Spectres. Tanks were separated from infantry, as they were at An Loc, and many were picked off with M72 LAWs. Another major invasion by 20 tanks and 5,000 infantry was launched on May 24, penetrating the city's defenses. As at An Loc, it was preceded by an apocalyptic artillery barrage and tanks firing directly into the command bunker. Two tanks were destroyed with M72 LAWs, while *Hawk's Claw* helicopters knocked out five more. The resident US advisors and senior ARVN colonels escaped to the perimeter, where the ARVN survivors fought on.

The remaining South Vietnamese troops from the 44th Infantry Regiment tasked with defending Kontum were saved from defeat by the timely appearance of Cobras, which fired into the NVA force and separated the infantry from six accompanying T-54s. Both *Hawk's Claw* Hueys then arrived with more Cobras, destroying four T-54s with a single missile each and forcing the surviving two to hide in wrecked buildings.

After AH-1Gs dispersed the infantry assault, the remaining tanks attempted to regroup. They were harassed by Cobras, which also concentrated their fire on several 12.7mm AAA sites. M72 LAWs demolished one of the T-54s and an AC-130 knocked out the other one.

The NVA's tank force lost four vehicles to the TOW team on May 25, while on the 26th Cobras destroyed enemy-occupied buildings near Kontum airfield. By May 30 the two UH-1Bs had accounted for 25 tanks, all but four by crews commanded by CWOs Douglas Hixson and Daniel G. Rowe, together with three APCs, several trucks and artillery pieces, and numerous supply bunkers. Of 162 TOWs fired, 124 were successful.

However, reinforcements continued to pour in. By late May the NVA had occupied half of Kontum and was closing in on the command bunker – eight more tanks were destroyed during the defense of the latter. From May 28, the USAF began *Combat Skyspot* radar-directed attacks and sorties by 8th Tactical Fighter Wing (TFW) F-4 Phantom IIs armed with laser-guided bombs (LGBs). The unit targeted the NVA every 20 minutes in an attempt to break up the massive onslaught, bad weather having grounded other TACAIR assets. When conditions improved, Cobras and A-37Bs resumed combat operations, pounding NVA positions in northern Kontum, assisted by *Arc Light* bombing within 2,100ft of ARVN positions. In two days AH-1Gs fired 3,000 rockets, eliminating several NVA vehicles and killing more than 70 troops near the frontline. RVNAF A-1 Skyraiders, meanwhile, effectively targeted artillery and AAA positions. Mercifully, Strela missiles did not appear.

A major effort was also undertaken to strangle enemy supply lines and routes. The 17th Aviation Group (Combat) used 14 AH-1Gs and another four from H/17th Air Cavalry to support a force of Hueys, scouts, and lift helicopters in locating suitable targets for air strikes. At Kontum, the ARVN gradually re-took areas of the city, and the supply interdiction effort began to starve the enemy of fuel, ammunition, and food. In a particularly wounding attack, Cobras struck an NVA-occupied building directly opposite the ARVN HQ bunker, killing 122 enemy troops.

The TOW team left on June 22, handing the NUH-1Bs to the Cobra units of the 17th Aviation Group (Combat). AH-1G crews would continue to provide essential cover to the highly successful *Hawk's Claw* Hueys in-theater until the helicopters' departure from South Vietnam. The group's Cobra-equipped 361st AWC was specifically tasked with suppressing groundfire for attacking NUH-1Bs. Should one of the latter fall victim to AAA or an SA-7, the AH-1G crews on scene had to provide close protection for the downed *Hawk's Claw* helicopter in order to prevent its crew and TOW technology being captured.

By May 31, the ill-advised NVA assault on Kontum had been repelled. More than 4,000 communist troops and 80 tanks had been lost. Although some companies had been reduced in strength to fewer than 20 men, they were refused permission to withdraw. Kontum had been saved by air power and the courageous resistance of a small number of ARVN troops from the 44th Infantry Regiment.

From August 1972 US Army Cobra units were withdrawn from South Vietnam. This process concluded in January 1973 when the 20th ARA flew its Cobras to Saigon for shipment to the USA. Although US Army Hueys were left behind for the ARVN, no AH-1Gs were handed over.

STATISTICS AND ANALYSIS

The Vietnam War was the proving ground for the helicopter gunship and, in particular, Bell's Cobra, which completed more than a million hours of operational flying. Its combat debut also showed that, in the words of a 101st Airborne report, "The armed helicopter and fixed-wing fighter-bomber form a natural, effective fighting team. [It] flies underneath ceilings measured in hundreds of feet to locate targets."

When the defenses were prohibitive, tactical jets could deliver ordnance from higher, safer altitudes. Overall, 70 percent of tank kills were by gunships or tactical aircraft. Where tanks were exposed in open country, 8th TFW Phantom IIs with LGBs directed by a wingman F-4D or a *Pave Nail* OV-10A were successful, but most TACAIR kills against armor were with standard 500lb bombs. AC-130 *Pave Aegis* gunships from Ubon Royal Thai Air Force Base could also be particularly destructive. Such an aircraft was kept over An Loc constantly during the defense of the town. One example, flown by Capt Russell Olsen, destroyed five tanks attempting to overrun an ARVN firebase at Tan Canh and then took out seven T-54s at Dak To during the same mission.

Conversely, helicopter losses were huge. More than 13,000 were sent to Vietnam between 1961–72 and 5,086 were destroyed while accumulating more than seven million combat hours. The peak year was 1970, when 3,926 US Army helicopters (including 470 AH-1Gs) were in Vietnam. Overall losses reflected the difficulty of the terrain, weather, mechanical failure, and the vagaries of fate in that 2,282 of the 4,128 helicopters destroyed before 1971 were operational losses against 1,846 combat casualties.

Although no Cobras are known to have been shot down by tank crews, the losses to ground fire and AAA were heavy, including this F Battery, 3/1st Cavalry AH-1G which was flying low to engage a tank near An Loc. Combat losses accounted for 173 Cobras, with a further 112 destroyed in operational accidents. (US Army)

Helicopter skeptics in the early 1960s asserted that rotary-winged craft would be sitting ducks over any defended areas of operation. In South Vietnam, specifically at Kontum and An Khe, Cobras fought at close quarters amid extraordinarily intense AAA with minimal losses. The introduction of SA-7s was a significant theat, but even they were largely overcome by the employment of effective countermeasures.

By January 1970, 12 percent of the US Army helicopters in South Vietnam were AH-1Gs and 20 percent OH-6As. The subsequent withdrawal of US forces in-theater saw the number of combat troops decline to 6,000 by March 30, 1972. They comprised the 3rd Brigade of the 1st Cavalry (Airmobile) and two battalions of the 196th Infantry Brigade, and all were scheduled to depart that year. Eventually, only 26 officers from the large Team 33 of US advisors remained, along with troops primarily tasked with guarding airfields. The final armored unit of the 1st Cavalry headed home in April 1972, by which point Hanoi's propaganda was urging a major attack on South Vietnam. The 7/17th Air Cavalry's B and C Troops were preparing to depart when the Easter Offensive began. Their orders were promptly reversed.

Although helicopter losses were severe, they had to be considered in the context of the vast numbers of sorties flown and the amplitude of the AAA defenses, which were far more numerous and well-prepared than expected. In 26,126,070 combat sorties flown from 1967 to 1970, only one helicopter was destroyed for every 19,599 sorties. Cobra units flew 19,235 sorties overall, averaging up to 804 per day with 57 aircraft. Only 18 AH-1G were lost during that period, two of them in sapper attacks on Khe Sanh. Cobras sustained 71 hits by 12.7mm guns during that operation and survived 92 percent of them.

Their expenditure of ordnance was formidable. From February to July 1972, 79th ARA Cobras fired 23,056 rockets and 187,500 rounds of 7.62mm ammunition. However, the unit also lost a third of its aircrew during that period. The loss of 27 helicopters (primarily UH-1s) at one LZ (*Lolo*) in *Lam Son 719* demonstrated the requirement for better protection for airborne assault forces. It also became clear that Cobras needed more effective rocket or missile armament when it came to knocking out tanks. This meant that the enemy's mass assaults at An Loc and Kontum could not be defeated by helicopter gunships alone, with the "heavy hammer" of *Arc Light*s and TACAIR doing the real damage that blunted such attacks.

A series of massive deployments provided reinforcement for the remaining US air assets in the area, while ground troop numbers continued to decline. In May 1972, as a result of the Easter Offensive, several wings of tactical aircraft were rapidly deployed to bases in Thailand and South Vietnam. By May 30, there were 348 USAF F-4/RF-4

ARVN 8th Infantry Regiment troops observe T-54Bs entering southern An Loc in June 1972. (US Army)

Phantom IIs, 171 B-52s (some flying from Guam), 28 AC-119 and AC-130 gunships, and numerous F-105Gs, A-37Bs, rescue helicopters, and A-1 Skyraiders operating from airfields in Southeast Asia. US Army aviators were quick to acknowledge that their successes in 1972 relied on the parallel efforts of TACAIR and B-52s from Strategic Air Command.

Most of the NVA's 134 T-54, 56 PT-76 and an undisclosed number of T-34 tanks eliminated in this campaign were indeed destroyed by tactical aircraft, often called in to strike tank targets that were detected by helicopter gunship crews who were unable to bring appropriate weapons to bear on them. USAF F-4s with LGBs were particularly effective against armor and AAA, with six tanks being destroyed by Mk 84s and two with M118s. A direct hit was needed to wreck a T-54, although they could be knocked out (by removing a track, for example) by "dumb" bombs – 11 tanks were destroyed with such ordnance, and a 12th by a CBU-24 cluster bomb unit (CBU). The combination of Mk 82 GP bombs and Mk 27 napalm was responsible for the destruction of 28 tanks. Four more were destroyed by five-inch Zuni rockets with 15lb shaped charge warheads in just four attacks by US Navy/US Marine Corps aircraft, while CBU-24 and Mk 20 Rockeye CBUs from US Navy aircraft were used in 49 attacks, destroying 11 tanks.

In the estimation of 101st Airborne analysts, the loss of so much armor "denied the NVA a critical advantage" over South Vietnamese forces and severely impeded the tank regiments' effectiveness. While its rigid command structures and adherence to plans denied local commanders flexibility, the NVA's armor strategy was invariably more purposeful than the ARVN's. The Easter Offensive had required most of North Vietnam's military capacity, and the losses suffered took three years to remedy. US Army Intelligence calculated that the NVA had lost half of its tanks by June 1972. However, North Vietnam had conquered territory that it retained after the ceasefire.

At An Loc, with extremely heavy, concentrated AAA, only three Cobras were lost in 6,473 sorties. As the 3rd Regional Assistance Command after-action report commented in its acknowledgment that not all rocket attacks succeeded, "Not one [Cobra] was destroyed by a tank, or even hit while engaging a tank." At An Loc, it was estimated that 80 of the 118 tanks fielded by the NVA were lost. As Gen Creighton Abrams observed, the North Vietnamese were willing to continue attacks with "an inherent acceptance that the forces involved may be expended totally."

AFTERMATH

The Cobra units' pioneering work guaranteed the armed helicopter a central role in post-Vietnam armies throughout the world. However, by 1970, the AH-1G's survivability was already being questioned, with increasing threats from missiles in Vietnam and more numerous and advanced defenses in the European theater, where it was still most likely that Cobras would have to resist formidable Soviet armored divisions. Without stand-off or precision guided weapons, that task, as Vietnam showed, had become too challenging. The success of *Hawk's Claw* TOW missions reinforced the Cobra's need for better anti-tank armament, but the war ended before those systems could be tested and deployed with units. In the mid-1960s, an AH-1G had in fact been tested with the Rockwell AGM-64 Viper missile which was later developed into the anti-armor AGM-114 Hellfire in 1974.

As production of the AH-1G for the US Army, US Marine Corps, and Spain neared 1,500 in 1972, the AAFSS decision was still open. An unforeseen consequence of *Lam Son 719* was that its outcome hastened the demise of the AH-56 Cheyenne. In 1971 Gen William Moyer, a persistent critic of the project, argued in a Congressional hearing that the losses in that battle proved that the assault helicopter concept had failed. Many accepted this distorted view and, combined with energetic lobbying from Bell Helicopters and the crash of the AH-56 prototype, Cheyenne funding was ended.

However, the US Army still needed a follow-up to the "interim" Cobra, and in November 1972 it announced a new Advanced Attack Helicopter program which would lead to the Hughes Model 77 – the YAH-64 Apache – in September 1975. Bell's YAH-63 was the only rival, but the Apache was selected in 1976.

Meanwhile, Bell continued to develop its AH-1, producing prototypes of the Model 309 King Cobra with a single engine (an improved AH-1G). The US Marine Corps, meanwhile, needed twin engines for additional safety in its carrier-deployable

AH-1J Sea Cobra. The AH-1J used a linked pair of Pratt & Whitney T400-CP-400 "Twin-Pac" turboshaft engines, and this was the only significant structural alteration to the basic AH-1G. The "Twin-Pac" provided an additional 400shp at the same gross weight of 10,000lb as the AH-1G. AH-1J development led to several later variants, including the longer AH-1T, the more powerful AH-1W Super Cobra and the AH-1Z with a four-bladed rotor, many of which still remain in service with several nations in 2024.

The most obvious upgrade for the AH-1G as a tank killer was to equip it with the M56 TOW missile system which had been so successful with the experimental *Hawk's Claw* UH-1B contingent in 1972. Bell's Improved Cobra Armament Program in March 1972 adapted the AH-1G to carry TOWs in single missile, two- or four-tube launcher units. Initially, eight aircraft redesignated YAH-1Qs were equipped with the Bell-Hughes M26 Telescopic Sight Unit above the nose turret and two four-shot M56 packs. Each missile had a pair of infrared flares on its tail that had to be tracked by the gunner visually with a Stabilized Multisensor Sight. Extensive test firings were conducted between 1973–75, and the US Army ordered 101 AH-1Gs to be converted into BGM-71A TOW-capable AH-1Qs.

AH-1G production ended in January 1973. It was followed by an order for 189 new-build AH-1Q/TOW Cobras on December 16, 1974, the new variants

Cobra evolution involved the conversion of 387 AH-1Gs to AH-1Fs from 1988, incorporating improvements from the AH-1P/ Q/S. Flat-paned canopies replaced the original type and an M197 20mm cannon and TOW missile capability were introduced, together with the M147 Rocket Management System to enable 2.75in. rockets to be fired. (DPLA/Public Domain)

distinguishable by their flat-paned canopies (with seven flat transparencies) introduced in the AH-1P, reducing radar signature and sun glint.

Tests showed that the 500lb extra weight of the two-tube TOW system and its associated equipment and structural strengthening left the AH-1G conversions short of power for the strenuous maneuvers needed to hunt tanks at low altitude. Through a 1975 US Army program for Improved Cobra Agility and Maneuverability, the AH-1Q was retrofitted with the more powerful 1,800shp Lycoming turboshaft and revised drivetrain, resulting in 92 AH-1Qs and 198 AH-1Gs being redesignated AH-1Ss from 1976.

The US Army now had the dedicated tank destroyer that would have punished NVA armored units more heavily. The AH-1S version became the standard anti-armor helicopter in frontline service in Europe in the late 1970s. A final modernization occurred in 1988 when the US Army purchased 530 AH-1Fs. This "modernized AH-1S" was externally similar to the original S-model, but it had considerable equipment updates including a new fire control system, a computer and laser rangefinder, an M76 head-up display, a new infrared countermeasures unit, and secure voice communications. The AH-1G was the basis of most AH-1Fs, with 387 being converted for service alongside 193 newly built examples with the US Army and Army National Guard.

Numerous armed forces have late-production AH-1s or AH-64s as their primary anti-armor weapons, and both types have played important roles in many post-Vietnam conflicts, including Operations *Desert Storm*, *Enduring Freedom*, and *Iraqi Freedom*. The use of armed helicopters against heavy armor was validated once again in the summer of 2023 when Russian Federation Kamov Ka-52M Alligator attack helicopters responded to the first stages of the Ukrainian counter-offensive. Firing their 9K121 Vikhr anti-armor missiles from positions beyond the range of Ukrainian man-portable air defense systems, the Alligators inflicted a heavy toll on Ukrainian main battle tanks at the forward edge of the battlefield.

FURTHER READING

BOOKS

Bernstein, Jonathan, *Osprey Combat Aircraft 41 – US Army AH-1 Cobra Units in Vietnam* (Osprey Publishing, 2003)

Bowden, Mark, *Huê 1968* (Grove Press, 2018)

Brennan, John, *Vietnam War Helicopter Nose Art* (Fonthill Media LLC, 2017)

Brennan, John, *Vietnam War Helicopter Art Volume 2* (Stackpole Military Photo Series, 2014)

Brown, Mike, *Missile, Missile, Missile!* (CreateSpace Independent Publishing Platform, 2013)

Childers, Jerry W., *Without Parachutes* (AuthorHouse 2005)

Chinnery, Philip D., *Vietnam – The Helicopter War* (Airlife Publishing, 1991)

Davies, Peter E., *Osprey Duel 112 – UH-1 Huey Gunship vs NVA/VC Forces* (Osprey Publishing, 2021)

Duong, Van Nguyen, *Inside An Loc*, (McFarland & Company, 2016)

Garrison, Mark, *Guts 'n Gunships* (Amazon, 2015)

Grandolini, Albert, *The Easter Offensive, Vietnam 1972 Volumes 1 and 2* (Helion, 2015)

Hartley, Robert F., *Gunship Pilot* (Liferich Publishing, 2015)

Heistand, William E., *Osprey New Vanguard 303 – Tanks in the Easter Offensive 1972* (Osprey Publishing, 2022)

Jennings, Lew, *19 Minutes to Live* (Amazon, 2017)

Johnson, Lawrence H., *Winged Sabres* (Stackpole Books, 1990)

Lanning, Michael Lee and Cragg, Dan, *Inside the VC and the NVA* (Texas A&M University Press, 2008)

Marvicsin, Dennis J. and Greenfield, Jerold A., *Maverick* (G. P. Putnam's Sons, 1990)

Mason, Robert, *Chickenhawk* (Corgi Books, 1984)

Melson, Charles D., *Osprey Campaign 362 – Vietnam 1972: Quang Tri* (Osprey Publishing, 2021)

Mesko, Jim, *Airmobile* (Squadron/Signal, 1984)

Mills, Hugh L. with Anderson, Robert A., *Low Level Hell* (Orion Publishing Group, 1992)

Peeters, Willy, *Lock On No. 6 – AH-1S Cobra* (Verlinden Publications, 1989)

Rottman, Gordon L., *Osprey Elite 154 – Vietnam Airmobile Warfare Tactics* (Osprey Publishing, 2007)

Scutts, Jerry, *UH-1 Iroquois/AH-1 Cobra* (Ian Allan, 1984)

Sheehan, Neil, *A Bright Shining Lie* (Pan Books, 1989)

Stanton, Shelby L., *Anatomy of a Division* (Presidio Press, 1987)

Thi, Lam Quang, *Hell in An Loc*, (University of North Texas Press, 1972)

Verier, Mike, *Osprey Air Combat – Bell AH-1 Cobra* (Osprey Publishing, 1990)

Whitley, Kenneth and Lalli, M.J., *Hovering Horizons* (Adler and Holmes LLC, 2020)

Willbanks, James H., *The Battle of An Loc* (Indiana University Press, 2005)

Zahn, Randy R., *Snake Pilot*, (Potomac Books, 2003)

Zaloga, Steven J., *Osprey New Vanguard 102 – T-54 and T-55 Main Battle Tanks 1944–2004* (Osprey Publishing, 2004)

DOCUMENTS

AH-1 Cobra Technical Manual TM 55-1520-236-10 1980 (Department of the Army, Washington, DC)

CHECO/CORONA Report – 1972 Invasion of Military Region 1

CHECO Report – The Battle for An Loc

Thiet Gap! The Battle of An Loc April 1972 by Lt Col James H. Willbanks (Combat Studies Institute, 1993)

After Action Reports by a variety of units from 1970–72 including the 1/9th Cavalry, 17th Air Cavalry, 17th ACS, 129th AHC, 101st Air Cavalry, 229th AHB and 361st Aviation Company

INDEX

Page numbers in **bold** refer to illustrations. Some caption locators are in brackets.